THE HARP OF GLORY

Enzira Sebhat

ST VLADIMIR'S SEMINARY PRESS
Popular Patristics Series
Number 39

The Popular Patristics Series published by St Vladimir's Seminary Press provides readable and accurate translations of a wide range of early Christian literature to a wide audience—students of Christian history to lay Christians reading for spiritual benefit. Recognized scholars in their fields provide short but comprehensive and clear introductions to the material. The texts include classics of Christian literature, thematic volumes, collections of homilies, letters on spiritual counsel, and poetical works from a variety of geographical contexts and historical backgrounds. The mission of the series is to mine the riches of the early Church and to make these treasures available to all.

Series Editor
BOGDAN BUCUR

Associate Editor
IGNATIUS GREEN

* * *

Series Editor
1999–2020
JOHN BEHR

The Harp of Glory: Enzira Sebhat

AN ALPHABETICAL HYMN OF PRAISE
FOR THE EVER-BLESSED VIRGIN MARY
FROM THE ETHIOPIAN ORTHODOX CHURCH

Introduced and Translated from the
Latin Version of M. Van Oudenrijn O.P.
Corpus Scriptorum Christianorum Orientalium
vol. 40. Louvain 1961.
by

JOHN ANTHONY MCGUCKIN

ST VLADIMIR'S SEMINARY PRESS
YONKERS, NEW YORK
2010

Library of Congress Cataloging-in-Publication Data

Enzira Sebhat. English.

The harp of glory : an alphabetical hymn of praise for the ever-blessed Virgin Mary from the Ethiopian Orthodox Church / introduced and translated from the Latin version of M. Van Oudenrijn O.P., Corpus Scriptorum Christianorum Orientalium, vol. 40, Louvain, 1961, by John Anthony McGuckin.

    p. cm. — (Popular patristics series ; no. 39)

    "Enzira sebhat."

    ISBN 978-0-88141-054-9

    1. Mary, Blessed Virgin, Saint—Devotion to. 2. Ya'ltyopya 'ortodoks tawahedo béta kerestiyan—Hymns. I. McGuckin, John Anthony. II. Title.

BT645.E5913 2010
242'.74—dc22

2010029897

COPYRIGHT © 2010 BY

ST VLADIMIR'S SEMINARY PRESS
575 Scarsdale Road, Yonkers, NY 10707
1-800-204-2665
www.svspress.com

ISBN 978-0-88141-054-9
ISSN 1555-5755

PRINTED IN THE UNITED STATES OF AMERICA

Contents

For My Beloved Eileen

Introduction

This great Ethiopian poem, in praise of the Blessed Mother of God and Ever Virgin Mary, known as the *Enzira Sebhat* (*The Harp of Glory*)[1] is no less than an "African Akathist." It matches that great Byzantine rhapsody both in artistic quality and religious fervor, and is offered here to the Orthodox faithful as a veritable gem, found in, and taken from, a treasure chest that has been so rarely opened by the wider Christian world. Ethiopian Orthodox spirituality remains an unknown element to most of the Latin, Byzantine, or wider Christian worlds. And that is a matter of ecumenical sadness, as well as being a lost opportunity. For although many Orthodox might tend to think first of the Christological divisions which have sprung up after, and on account of, the Council of Chalcedon in 451,[2] it might be a more appropriate thing to think more generously of the great antiquity and profound spirituality of the worlds of the Coptic and Ethiopic churches, arenas of Christian life and deeply tested

[1] The Ethiopian title literally means the *Lyre of Praise*, but the author himself decides to entitle his work *Harp of Glory* in his prologue strophe.

[2] The Coptic and Ethiopian churches not subscribing to the Chalcedonian confession of two natures ineffably united in the single divine person of the Lord, but holding to an earlier iteration (of St. Cyril of Alexandria) of the "Single nature (*Mia Physis*) of God the Word made flesh." In 433, in a confession of faith arranged by the Patriarchate in Constantinople, one designed to reconcile the Syrian church, St. Cyril himself moved from his earlier confession of the *Mia Physis* to the acceptance of the two natures (*dyo physeis*) ineffably united in the single divine person of the Lord (which Chalcedon later ratified), and clearly regarded both positions as theologically equivalent, even though appearing to adopt contradictory terms (the word *physis* had a range of different meanings in antiquity). In recent years there have been encouraging discussions of Christological belief between the Eastern and Oriental Orthodox churches on this major question. For a fuller background, cf. J.A. McGuckin. *St. Cyril of Alexandria and the Christological Controversy* (Crestwood, NY: St Vladimir's Seminary Press, 2001).

experience, for these churches are veritable cradles of martyrs. What
we may call the "ethos" of this Christian world, is so filled with the
living spirit of Orthodoxy because it is founded on so many of the
same liturgical springs, and so many shared authoritative Fathers of
the Church, as those of the Orthodox Church.

In its history and tradition Ethiopia knew, and preserved, a deep
Alexandrian, a Syrian, as well as a Byzantine theological influence,
all fundamental influences that were the foundations of the theological traditions of the Orthodox Church. In its devotion to the
Blessed Virgin, Ethiopia fashioned its sources in accordance with
the ancient styles of Greek *encomia*, or hymns of praise, but made
of them something uniquely its own, and quintessentially African.
The Harp of Glory, translated here, quite obviously "absorbed" the
Byzantine Akathist at some stage in its pre-history, but what emerges
is something uniquely new. The poetry, as it were, bears a direct
relation to Byzantine forms, but is painted in distinctive and radiant
earth-colors taken from the highlands of Africa, and imbued with
different perfumes, redolent of the cinnamon, incense, and balsamic
pine which the poet refers to so often in his lines.

The learned Dominican priest Mark Van den Oudenrijn, prepared the critical edition of the *Enzira Sebhat* for the series *Corpus
Scriptorum Christianorum Orientalium* (CSCO).[3] It appeared in vol.
208 of the CSCO for the year 1960, and was subtitled as vol. 39 of the
series *Scriptores Aethiopici*, the volume dedicated to the "Prayers and
Hymns" assigned to Queen Helen. In the following year volume 40
of the *Scriptores Aethiopici* appeared (again within the aegis of volume 208 of CSCO) containing the literal Latin version prepared by
Van den Oudenrijn of the Ethiopic text. It is from his Latin, a close
following of the original Ge'ez, that the present English rendering
has been made, the first appearance, at least so I believe, of this great
Ethiopian masterpiece in English.

[3]*Corpus Scriptorum Christianorum Orientalium,* published by the Catholic
University of Louvain.

In the fifteenth century the Cult of the Virgin Mary reached new heights in Ethiopia. It flourished in the aftermath of the cruel suppression of a wide variety of Ethiopian Christian customs and practices, which King Constantine (Zar'a Ya'qob, 1433–1468) had ordered in the cause of rooting out heresies and bringing his church and country to a new harmony and order from which to face the growing power of Islam. After his time many books of "Salutations"[4] of the Blessed Virgin were composed by the clergy and enjoyed a wide popularity among the people. Zar'a Ya'qob also instructed that the reading of the *Book of the Miracles of Our Lady Mary* should henceforth be read in the churches, and so Marian devotion entered into the regular liturgical cycle of the Ethiopian church. The liturgical year in Ethiopia soon numbered no less than thirty-three major Marian festivals, and thus far outnumbered even the Byzantine calendar's extensive devotion to the Virgin. King Zar'a Ya'qob is believed to have composed theological treatises himself, in the manner of an emperor Justinian. And several of his royal successors also had hymns ascribed to them.

The two poems contained in vol. 39 of *Scriptores Aethiopici, The Harp of Glory* (*Enzira Sebhat*) and *The Gate of Light* (*Hohta Berhan*), were customarily ascribed to Queen Helen, who reigned at the end of the fifteenth and beginning of the sixteenth centuries. The ascription, however, is a nominal one, for the poem itself gives abundant indications that it was written by a monastic and certainly by a male composer. Ascription to a royal author was a common trope among courtly writers in Ethiopia. Moreover, both these titles of the books are extensively used in Ethiopic literature, and one cannot be sure that whenever they are alluded to any single specific "work" can be presumed. They are, first and foremost, titles of the Blessed Virgin herself, who was, herself, the "Gate of Light"[5] (through which came the Light of the World) and the "Harp of Glory," who in her own life

[4]Comparable to the *Chairetismoi* of the Byzantine tradition, of which the *Akathist* is the highest example.

[5]cf. Ezek 44.2–3. The East Gate of the mystical temple through which no man could pass, only God himself.

first sang the great song of the praises of God through Christ the Lord. When a reference is made, therefore, to the "Harp of Glory," it is more than possible that it refers generically to a hymn that addresses the Blessed Virgin. That is, a "Harp of Glory" is comparable to what is known as a *Theotokion* in the Byzantine vocabulary, and originally covering any *encomium* that takes the Virgin as its subject.

The text, as we have noted, does not itself suggest a female, or even a royal author, and to the contrary has every indication of being the work of a monastic priest. The final strophe gives the name of the scribe as Hensa Krestos, but in such a way that while this final verse could well have been added by someone who was merely the scribe of the manuscript, it also seems to be integral to the epilogue as a whole that immediately precedes it, and where the actual author (and it is clearly him) explains his system of composition by arranging the verses according to the series of letters and different vocalisations. If this is so, then we have the actual composer's name attached, not merely that of the scribe, and the "traditional" attribution to Queen Helena has served simply to obscure the obvious.

Liturgical analogies abound, with constant reference to the Blessed Virgin Mary as the temple court, or the priestly vesture, which shelters the devoted servant of her and her son. The author frequently prays to the Virgin to "remember him who beseeches you," and the typical monastic prayer for protection against the "wiles of seductive women" gives a clear enough indication of its most likely origin from a monk-musician, perhaps one that was attached to the court, for on several occasions there are final verses appealing to the Virgin to ensure safety for the borders of the kingdom, and reminding the hearers that it is devotion to the Virgin which secures the stability of the throne. The author of the poem, then, himself dedicated to chastity, seeks after the Virgin's blessing "so as to live within the nuptial chamber of her inner house." The central image, ostensibly erotic, mirrors the style of the secular love song written by court troubadours, but is here taken into the vocabulary of the ascetics on the loose model of the *Song of Songs* (or

Canticles, which provides a recurring fund of imagery, and runs like a river through the whole length of this poem), and especially as this had been inducted into Christian mystical teaching, following the lead given by Origen of Alexandria in his celebrated *Commentary on the Song of Songs*, in which he was the first (of many to come) to interpret the longing of the beloved and her lover, as a symbol of the Christian soul seeking after the delight of the love of the Holy Logos incarnate in Jesus.

Mary's nuptial chamber is thus the inner place in the eschatological household of virgins, the secret place reserved for the chaste who love her Son, an image of the eschatological church of the elect. *The Harp of Glory*, therefore, was a poem written in the style of the Byzantine *Erotikon*[6], but applied as an extended analogy of the quest for the love of God in the ascetic life; a love that was fired, and protected, by a total commitment to Christ mediated through self-dedication to Mary the Virgin. One can imagine the scene of the delivery of such a composition, for it often refers to the need for the devout "to run to the hallways of Mary early in the dawn." Harp-playing (the portable African lyre is meant) was one of the attributes of the monastics of Ethiopia, a practice following in the footsteps of the lyre-playing King David who traditionally sang his great biblical poems, the Psalms, to that accompaniment. Wandering monk-troubadours would take their music far and wide, evangelizing and catechizing the people, at the same time as entertaining them. Liturgically, the poem also enjoyed popularity as part of the service of day-dawn praises, comparable to the manner in which, in Byzantine liturgical custom, the final canons of the Matins service are dedicated to the Blessed Theotokos. But it surely had a wider application, just as the Byzantine *Akathist* hymn itself had a wider popular origin as a street processional before it became restricted to its use in Orthodox Lenten liturgical devotions.

[6]The secular love song. This was exactly what the great Byzantine poet, Symeon the New Theologian, did in his own Hymns of Divine Eros, a few centuries before the composition of the *Harp of Glory*.

The poem is essentially a vast biblical carpet of references. Such a monumental weight of allusions is not accidental. The singer-composer, by the simple device of the form of a beautiful love song, is actually laying down the ground for an extended explanation of the typological understanding of the scriptures. A modern reader, used to interpreting the Bible according to its sequential narrative content, and its historical or ethical significances, is singularly ill-equipped to realize that throughout the vast majority of Christian history this is *not* how the Bible was generally read. In earlier Christian ages (and the style still applies predominantly to most of the Bible as it appears in Church in the form of liturgical poetry) the scripture was read in fragmented pericopés, each one turning around a Type (*tupos*): namely a figure or symbol or story from the old text that was reworked symbolically in line with the evangelical mystery. So, for example, the old story of Abraham and Isaac's sacrifice[7] becomes, by reference to the inherent symbols of the "Beloved Son" carrying "the wood" (the Cross) of his own sacrifice "up the hill" (Calvary), for the establishment of "a new covenant" of grace (the foundation of New Israel) in the hands of the Christian readers of antiquity, a story "substantively" referred to the significance of the death and resurrection of Jesus. Type, in this case, means that this reference to the passion-covenant theology is "really" what the Abrahamic story is all about. Its "other meaning" (what one might call the literal or first-sight meaning, as something to do with the patriarchs and the establishment of the covenant with Israel) was understood as a level of revelation on the surface, meant to be passed through by the enlightened reader (the one who had been given the key to the mystical interpretation through the acceptance of the Gospel story).

The mechanism of this form of interpretation was based upon three central notions common among the Fathers of the Church[8]

---

[7]Gen 22.1–18.

[8]Origen of Alexandria was the first to put together the format of the global theory, and the later Fathers (it was primarily a work of St. Gregory of Nazianzus and St. Basil the Great) salvaged principles by gathering them into the *Philocalia of Origen*, which gave them vast dissemination through the early and medieval Church.

namely: that (a) all scripture was a single inter-related text telling the same story of the Incarnate Word; (b) that all scripture had superficial levels of meaning that deepened in a mystical significance made visible according to the initiation possessed by the disciple of Christ; and (c) that there were clues within the text, at surface level, that gave signs to the initiate reader who would read the old story (the Old Testament) "back from the new,"[9] not forward as if reading historically.[10] Like the "type" of an old machine-press, which was reversed so that its impression on the paper would render the letters in their correct readable alignment, so too the biblical "type" was an enigmatic symbol, or story, hidden in the Old Testament whose "real meaning" became apparent to the careful (initiated) observer only in the light of the Gospel, and only according to the degree of the illumination which the Divine Spirit of God gave to the heart of the faithful reading it "In Christ."[11]

The poem can be recommended, apart from the inherent beauty of its praises of the Blessed Virgin, as a major window on how the Ethiopian Church read its sacred scriptures typologically (and thereby how most of Christian Antiquity did so too). Readers wishing to follow this exercise will find that, extensive though the

[9]Reading the Old Testament, that is, wholly, and entirely, in the light of the Gospel.

[10]Mar Theodore of Mopsuestia, described the issue succinctly in his argument that if the scripture is a sacred literature that transcends historicity, being of eschatological moment, then it cannot be exegeted solely by linear historical methods of interpretation.

[11]Reading the text, *en Christo* (1 Cor 4.10; 2 Cor 5.17; Eph 1.9) or with the "mind of Christ" *phronema Christou*, (cf. 1 Cor 2.13–16), it passes from simple textual reading to become a sacrament of divine revelation. The Church Fathers, then, believed that the Scripture really only became "sacred revelation" when it fulfilled that function in Christ, and through Christ. His was the presence that sanctified the literature and made it revelatory for the purpose of salvation. It was in this sense that Origen called the scripture, the "sacrament" of the body of the Logos. Further, see: J.A. McGuckin, "Recent Biblical Hermeneutics in Patristic Perspective: The Tradition of Orthodoxy," in T. Stylianopoulos, ed., *Sacred Text and Interpretation: Perspectives in Orthodox Biblical Studies. Papers in Honor of Prof. Savas Agourides* (Brookline, MA, Holy Cross Press: 2006), 293–324. [Also issued as a Special Issue of *Greek Orthodox Theological Review* 47.1–4 (2002)].

poem is, its profundity as a gateway to the Scripture is even more all-encompassing. The types that inform almost every line of the narrative, are not accidental or casual, rather they offer the key to interpretation of a massive array of biblical texts; in each case leading the reader to see the text anew in the light of the mystery of Christ's salvation of the world through the regal event of his Incarnation into time and space through the loving obedience of the Blessed Virgin. It is the Word's self-humbling to the order of time and space (his incarnate *kenosis*) and his exaltation (*anabasis*) in the heavenly glory of his philanthropy over the continuing world of humans and angels, which is the fundamental theme of this poem. The author takes the Blessed Virgin as herself the chief "type" of the incarnate redemption. Her Son's humility and glorification is mirrored in her own. She is emptied out as the obedient servant, and raised on high as "more honorable than the Cherubim, and more glorious beyond compare than the Seraphim."[12] Since all the world turns around the redemptive act of the Logos, and in this finds the very meaning of its creation, so too is the Virgin said to stand at the gate of all sacred history. For her sake, the Word made the world, drew together Israel, prepared the types of true worship, and sketched out the shape of the drama of salvation history. The poet sums it up most dramatically in his statement that it was "for her" that all Israel came to be.[13]

Readers from the Protestant tradition reading some of the praises of the Virgin in these pages might recoil, at some instances, from the way in which they seem to ascribe "too much," depicting her in words and terms that are only appropriate to the Divine Lord who was the "sole mediator" between God and man.[14] The author,

[12] As the Byzantine liturgy expresses it.

[13] By which, typically, he suggests the double typological figure of (a) the history of the patriarchs and matriarchs of Israelite history who are the ancestors of the Virgin, but who "run to her" as their glory; and also (b) the Virgin as the synopsis and symbol of the New Israel, the Church of Christ. She is the first and greatest of all the disciples, the one in whom all scripture is laid bare and manifest since she herself is the perfect crystalline vessel, purely reflective, of the Holy Spirit who filled her, and made of her something greater than any prophet, saint, or angel.

[14] 1 Tim 2.5.

however, is not being theologically careless, or letting his devotion to the Virgin run ahead of him, blurring the necessary distinction between the saints of the Lord, and the Lord of the saints. On the contrary, when the poet exalts the Blessed Virgin, he invariably does it as part of his understanding of the exaltation of the Lord himself and the diffusion of his resurrectional grace in the Church. The Blessed Virgin's light and radiance is not her own, it is that of the Father, the Word, and the Holy Spirit who so transfigured her, as the pure type of the redeemed disciple. The Trinitarian invocations at the head of each alphabetical section, where the author repeatedly states this, are not just tropes; they are fundamental to the author's theology. Mary is radiant and praiseworthy, because she is the demonstration to the world of what the resurrection glory of Christ will look like in the eschatological moment of the revelation of the perfect kingdom. But she is not a merely passive example of transfiguration. As her Divine Son passed through fire to become radiant in the resurrection, so too Mary was transfigured into greatness by passing through the crucible of obedience. Now, in her glory, the poet describes her as powerful and philanthropic, like her Son. Her eschatological glory is not a time of idleness, but a process wherein Virgin takes the initiative constantly to work beneficent *philanthropia* among the righteous of the Church. Almost at each moment (and certainly in the final verses of each strophe section throughout) the poet returns to his appeal to Mary as the Eschatological intercessor for the Church. She thus appears (as she does in the Byzantine Akathist and in most of the Marian literature of the Early Church) not as Mary the meek and mild maiden, but as the mighty Warrior Virgin, who is eager to help her kin, and crush the head of the serpent who still troubles the peace of the world.

All through the *Harp of Glory* the composer takes this ecclesiastical idiom of reading the scripture as a carpet of typology, for granted. The figure of Mary is praised by reference to all her types in the Old and New Testaments, and the range of them is so deep and extensive, that any one who followed them up by looking at the other significances of the larger stories from which the types were taken, would be left, at the end of the exegesis of this poem, with an encyclopedic knowledge of the Bible as it referred to the mystery of salvation in Christ. Thus, the poem served two functions; the first was to show Mary as the pathway to salvation in Christ. Devotion to her, far from being a distraction from the worship of her Son, is presented as a royal way to comprehension. The second theological theme flows from this, for the mother who in former times "pondered all these things in her heart"[15] is here presented as the great initiator of the deeper mysteries of Christ, and how his teaching and his meaning ebbs back and forth throughout all scripture, the Old as much as the New, as its heart and inner secret. It is the Virgin, as much as her Son, who is spoken of and prefigured in the ancient scriptures. She is the true Ark of the Covenant, the true Gate of the Temple, and so forth. Her glory is not a distraction from that of her Son (the great complaint of the Reformation world), on the contrary understanding her magnificence is the portico of the disciple's initiation into the true significance of Jesus. As the poet himself puts it:

> Blessed is he who keeps the way of your
>   commandments[16]
> And who proves himself an initiate of your Son's teaching;
> Under your shade will he rest,
> And in the nuptial chamber of your house will he be
>   received.

It clearly being understood that there is, and only can be, one single house, here; where disciples enter into rooms prepared for them in glory:[17] the house of Mary where she serves as gracious hostess, and covers the needs and embarrassments of those in want, just as she did when she was in attendance of Jesus in his ministry,[18] is the

[15]Lk 2.19, 51.
[16]Prov 6.32.
[17]Jn 14.2.
[18]Jn 2.3.

house of her Son, which in turn is none other than the house of the Father.

The poem is a work of great literary charm and imaginative genius. It is originally in the form of an extended alphabetical hymn. The present translation has represented this merely in a formal way (with an overrun of four letters coming after Z),[19] and I have to confess that sensible line *initia* for the X and the Y were beyond me; but in the Ethiopian, each stanza for each letter is developed with all the variant forms of the seven vocalizations relevant for each instance of the alphabet,[20] something, of course, that is impossible for the English.

The single manuscript of the *Enzira Sebhat* (*Codex Parisinus Abbadianus* 121) dates from the seventeenth or eighteenth centuries. The poem itself is older than this, possibly from as early as the fifteenth century revival of Marian hymns of salutation, presided over in this era by King Zar'a Ya'qob. Its thought-world, however, is certainly older still, and owes much to Byzantine theological and poetical forms, which were present in the Ethiopian church from ancient times.

Apart from its massive dedication to the theology of redemption, and its monumental witness to the typological understanding of the scriptures, what does the poem reveal to us incidentally? Among other things, the verses show a lively fear of magicians and the machinations of evil spirits and constantly seek the Virgin's protection against malign influences. There are also lots of prayers throughout for the faithful to be protected from uprisings of enemies–something that would have been particularly relevant in a Christian court which feared (and had every right to) the constant predations from the expanding Islamic society that surrounded it. All through the work there are signs of great political instability. It is this, of course, which has made the writing of the history of the Ethiopian Church

[19]The four letters are "AMEN," being the best I could think of since the English alphabet ran out.
[20]For example: Ha, Hu, Hi, Hâ, Hê, Hë, Ho.

such a difficult task, so many and so devastating have been the waves of attack and destruction that have over the many centuries, driven Christian Ethiopia up into the mountains and away from the littoral of the Gulf.

In the heart of the Ethiopian Christian the Virgin is appealed to as the "walled and fortified city that cannot be toppled." She is invoked to fulfill the recurring prayer of the psalmist that his enemies may be shattered and frustrated. The poet takes the *Psalter* and *Canticles* as his two major quarries for material. If we are surprised, when reading the poem, how he moves so smoothly from loving words of endearment, to outraged demands that the backs of his foes should be whipped, then it is the Psalter that explains it for us, as almost all his execrations of evil are lifted verbatim from there. On many occasions we move seamlessly from an appeal to "put down" the "enemies ranged against my soul" that seem to be military threats, and into enemies that are understood spiritually, as demonic influences and temptations to vice. This typological movement is common to much ancient literature among the Christians, and does not mean that only one or the other is to be understood: rather that the poet (an ascetic trying to live a peaceful life in the mastery of the passions) knows all too well that the violence of the "principalities of evil"[21] which he fears still dominate the world's affairs, is manifested unceasingly in external war and oppression, as well as in the interior of the soul of any who strive to live in that peace and righteousness which is so hateful to them. The poet appeals to the Virgin Mary as Queen of the angels, not in a merely rhetorical way, but as one who exactly believes that she is "more honorable than the Cherubim." Accordingly she is the mighty warrior spirit, who is greater even than Michael the Archangel.

She is a leader of the eschatological army that ever withstands the encroachment of evil on this world's plane. Without the backdrop, ever present, of this eschatological sense of battle and embattlement, it is impossible to understand the force of the poem. The poet is not

[21]Eph 6.12.

some dewy-eyed Pre-Raphaelite, offering "garlands of snowdrops" (one can think of some of the nineteenth century Ultramontane Marian hymns, and cringe); rather, he is a monastic priest fulfilling his duty, praying for the welfare of the world by invoking against the powerful forces of maleficent power in the world, the even more powerful assistance of the spirits of grace and goodness, headed by the Virgin as leader of the Redeemed. As is the case in the great narratives of the Old Testament, the whole story is woven through with the thread of threat and destruction, failure and oppression, as well as success and blessing. The same eschatological song is present in a pervasive way through the New Testament narrative too, though often it has been overlooked by readers who have preferred a simpler form of exegesis. The twentieth century, in particular, has had as its theme the "de-mythologization" of the scriptures, as if this would somehow make their meaning more clear. But, in many ways, it is comparable to excising the concept of war from Tolkien's *Lord of the Rings*,[22] and hoping to keep the narrative sense intact.

Lastly we may mention that the poem is deeply steeped in liturgical sensibility. Ethiopian liturgy is a rarely studied thing for Christians who do not belong to that tradition. But it is an exceptionally rich vein there. There are at least fourteen major *Anaphoras*, or Eucharistic prayers, still in use in the Church. The concept of the Ark of the Covenant is also very important to the Ethiopian Church, not least in the lively tradition that the Ark was not finally lost, but was brought from Jerusalem and found shelter among the Christians in the African highlands. Each Ethiopian Orthodox Church celebrates the Eucharist on a small model of the Ark that serves as its altar table. This might give some explanation of why the poet so often returns to the notion of the Blessed Virgin as the priestly Ephod, and the sacred vestments.[23] She is also the altar of incense, the golden vessels of the temple offerings, and so on. The concept of the Jerusalem temple,

---

[22]Itself a work deeply based on scriptural types. Tolkien was one of the English Catholic editors of the Jerusalem Bible, and a thoughtful theologian.

[23]Ex 28.1–43.

both as a reality, and as an eschatological symbol of renewal,[24] underpins the poet's understanding of the priestly role of the Virgin in the story of Christian redemption. The same idea, of course, is found in the Gospel of St. John, and elsewhere.[25] The Lord himself is the Temple of God's presence. But the poet continually turns on the idea that Mary was the containment of the Uncontainable God.[26] She held within the small space of her womb, him who was the Maker of the vast Heavens. She was like the Ark of the Covenant that held within it the uncontainable presence of God; or she was the Burning Bush that held within it, inconceivably so, the flames of fire that did not consume it; or she was the Holy of Holies, that was the place on earth where the Glory dwelt.

The theme of the Virgin Mary as the Temple precinct is the summation of all these ideas: in each case it refers to the reality of the new mode of presence of God that has come into the world after the Incarnation of the Logos. As such, The Virgin is celebrated as the true type of that to which all ancient Hebrew priesthood looked: the invocation of the presence of the Glory among Israel. For the author, Mary is the supreme priest, to whom all her long line of priestly ancestors looked, when they fulfilled the liturgical rites. She is robed in sanctity and purity, just as they were once robed in beauty. The presence of the Glory is within her, for she brought the Living God into the world of time and space. As the poet puts it dramatically: "For you bodily fashioned, Him who fashioned all." Apart from their intrinsic theological worth, I also take the constant liturgical and priestly references to be a clear sign that the poet was himself a monastic priest, much used to living and thinking in this modality. He regularly refers to his own work as an offering of incense, meant to rise up to heaven as an offering of thanks and praise. It was often the case that clerical ascetics would learn musical instruments for use in the African liturgy. The recitation of this hymn, known as

[24]As for example in Ezekiel 41–43.
[25]Jn 2.19–21; see also Rev 3.12 and 21.22.
[26]The Byzantine tradition of the *Theotokos Platytera*.

the *Enzira Sebhat* (*Lyre of Praise*) would, in all likelihood, in early times have been accompanied by that unforgettable lilting sound of the African lyre. Its public recitation would have been at one and the same moment: a liturgical event, a scriptural catechesis, and a great artistic performance. It is still used as a morning hymn of the Church.

It is with much pleasure that I am able now to share it with the larger readership it deserves.

Before passing to the text, let me finally state that in accordance with Orthodox church tradition, the multitude of Psalm references contained here are cited according to the Septuagintal numberings (LXX) as used in the liturgical books. This is the same numbering system as is found in most Catholic bibles, but differs from the Psalm numberings that will be found in Protestant versions of the bible which, since the time of the Reformation, have been based upon the Masoretic (Hebrew) text. To allow readers who do not have the LXX system in their bible versions to access the exact Psalm text the table of equivalence is as follows:

Greek Septuagint:	Hebrew
1–8	1–8
9	9–10
10–112	11–113
113	114–115
114–115	116
116–145	117–146
146–147	147
148–150	148–150.

For most of the psalms, then, the LXX numbering will be one psalm behind the Hebrew. The LXX also frequently begins the verse numbering with the psalm title (if it is more than a few words long) which in the Hebrew is not counted as part of the verses. In such cases verse one in the Hebrew numbering system will be verse 2 in the LXX. There is an additional problem for moderns wishing to check out the biblical references: one has to remember that the African theologian is consulting the Ge'ez text which has itself translated the Septuagintal version, as mediated through many centuries of liturgical usage. For these reasons, cross referencing the biblical references in the footnotes may often leave the reader puzzled. All I can say to that is the composer was not referencing a modern Protestant bible. The "odd discontinuities" that may sometimes occur between the reference as given and the text of the modern English versions such as the RSV, or comparable scholarly versions, are generally explicable on one or two bases: first the source text follows the Septuagintal (LXX) meaning not the Hebrew, and secondly, the text regularly alludes to the scripture rather than citing it exactly (a typical aspect of ancient church use of the holy texts). Names of prophets and places also follow the Septuagintal version via Ge'ez: all making for a wonderful sense of discovering something familiar that has been rendered into "something rich and strange."

John Anthony McGuckin.
Priest of the Romanian Orthodox Church.

Prologue

In the name of God the Father, who loved your beauty,[1]
And in the name of God the Son, who made you his tabernacle,
And in the name of God the Holy Spirit,
Who crowned you with the light of his glory and splendors,
So do I begin this song, which shall be called the "Harp of Glory"
    or the "Trumpet of Praise,"
And with an eager heart I sound out your exaltation on its strings.
I will progress through the order of letters, arranging them seven-
    fold,[2]
That my work might be an offering of glory to your name.
Grant eyes of wisdom and knowledge to my mind, O Virgin,
That it might gather the fruit of your praise from the Book of
    Paradise[3]
While, like a bee, I let my mind take flight on wings,
Gathering the flowers of your praises, harvesting their nectar,
So as to gladden your heart.
May this work find favor in your sight!

[1] Ps 44.12. Psalm references follow the Orthodox custom of the Septuagintal (LXX) numbering—generally one in advance of the Masoretic numbers (as used in Protestant editions of the Bible) and often one verse later. See the more detailed note on this at the end of the Introduction.

[2] The original Ethiopic text follows alphabetical letters in Ge'ez in sevenfold vowel distributions (the last three phonetic divisions are in quincunxes). I have marked the divisions nominally in English by seven paragraphs within the same alphabet letter A-Z, and a final "Amen."

[3] Sacred Scripture.

My Lady Mary—

*A*T night, and at the dawn of day, I bow before you,
Offering praise to that womb which contained the awesome
    radiance of God.
My Queen, humble in heart, and merciful of soul,
Raise me up from the sleep of indolence, to be a herald of your
    name.
Make me zealous and skilful in the cause of your praise,
Cast down upon me the great radiance of the light of your
    loveliness,
Let me never be cut off or exiled from your peaceful court.

My Lady Mary—
Gate of Peace from which the perfume of the spirit of life issues
    forth,
Which no wintry wind or rust can ever mar,
You are the House of Shem, which fell to him by lot, before his
    other brothers.[1]
You are that in which his father Noah's blessing was made
    effective.[2]
You are the Oak of Mamre where Abraham dwelt as an old man[3]
And whose shade contained the threefold God,[4]
When he made covenant with him, and all his seed thereafter.[5]

[1]Book of Jubilees 8.10f; Shem (in the Ark) is a type of Christ in the Virgin's womb.

[2]Mary is the Ark of salvation.

[3]Gen 18.4f.

[4]The revelation of the three angels at the Oak of Mamre (who are alternately designated as "Lords" and "Lord") is taken as a type of the revelation of One God who is Three. Containing one of the Trinity in her womb who is inseparable from the other divine persons, Mary is thereby (paradoxically) the one who contains the Uncontainable Trinity. In Byzantine tradition this is referred to as the *Theotokos Platytera* (the Mother of God "Wider-than-the Heavens").

[5]Gen 13.15.

You are that Fragrant Mountain of Isaac
Which produced the ram caught by its horns in the thorn bush.[6]
You are the Golden Ladder, on which the angels of the Most High
    ascended and descended,[7]
Which Jacob saw when he was in flight from his brother.
O Virgin, Holy Shrine of the heavenly God,
You are the Mount of Horeb in which His splendor appeared,
And on which His very feet were placed,[8]
When He made his law known to Jacob and his judgment to
    Israel.[9]
You are the Field of Araunah[10] in which David offered a sacrifice of
    salvation to his Maker,
When all his people were laid low under devastating plague.[11]
You are the Temple of Solomon whose inner chambers were filled
    with the glory of God,
On that occasion when the priests were unable to perform their
    service.[12]
You are that Cluster of Figs which became a healing poultice for
    Hezekiah[13]
When his days had come to an end, yet God added years to his life.
O Beautiful Lady, see how I have compared you to all manner of
    good and lovely things,
For the roots of the tree of your love are entwined within my heart,

[6] Gen 22.13.

[7] Gen 28.12.

[8] Deut 5.2, Exod17.6. The Sinai Theophany is a type of Mary's overshadowing by the Holy Spirit, and the incarnation within her of the Word of God.

[9] Ps 147.8(19).

[10] David bought Araunah's threshing floor to be the site of his sacrifice to God. It was outside the original City of David, and later became the site of the Temple of Solomon.

[11] 2 Sam 24. After David's sacrifice the plague was lifted from Israel. The episode becomes type of how Mary, as Temple of the divine presence, brings salvation to the world in the Incarnation.

[12] 1 Kg 8.11. The Cloud of Glory is a type of Mary, Shekinah of the presence of the Word.

[13] 2 Kg 20.7.

And that tree grows in stature and extends its branches to the
    shores of the sea of my mind.[14]
Its beauty has appeared like a flower upon my lips.
Anoint me then with fragrance from the perfume
Of your flower that has opened in bloom;
Its blood red color, from the side of your Son.
Through your prayers deliver me from the snares of Satan and all
    his deceitful arts.

My Lady Mary—
You are the Garden of Wisdom, whose flower does not fade or
    wither,
While the garden of the foolish quickly perishes and runs wild.
Beautiful Bride, your loveliness shines brighter than Orion,
    outshining the Sun in its beauty:
Light a lamp of knowledge and prudence in my heart.
Be ever watchful to protect me; ever ready to defend.

My Lady Mary—
Ark of the Covenant, clad in gold inside and out,[15]
Whose pillars the Cherubim covered on all sides;[16]
You are the Golden Table bordered with golden edges[17]
On which were placed the vessels for sacrifice.
You are the Candlestand[18] with the six branches;
Three on either side, casting light before and behind it.
You are the Dove of Prophecy, with silver wings,
Whose sides were chased with purest red-hued gold,[19]

[14]Cf. Ps 79.12.
[15]Ex 25.10f.
[16]Ex 25.18.
[17]Ex 25.23.
[18]Ex 25.32. The "Seven Branched Candle" made of pure gold, and set in the Temple, is described in the scripture (and here) as one lamp stand with six additional branches.
[19]Ps 68.13–14. The image in the Psalms refers to Israel in the type of a Dove, dressed in the sacred battle array for God's holy war (cf. Josh 22.8, Judg 8.24f.). The

Before whom the sons of Kore played their music in the gates of
     Sion.
O Virgin, do not set a curb upon my tongue,
Rather let it run even more nimbly, free of all constraints.

Lady Mary—
Mother of Our God Elohim,
You are glorified and honored on every side;
Wrapped in the robe of patience, and adorned in the vesture of
     clemency.
Light in my heart the radiant fire of the spirit of understanding,
That I might be always ready to praise you,
And most skilful in your celebration.

My Lady Mary—
Ewe-Sheep, Mother of the Gentle Lamb,
Beautiful Bride, radiant in countenance,[20] most pleasing to the
     Word,
I pray you watch over me from morning to evening,
And again from eventide to dawn of day.
Make me attentive in sounding your praises,
Industrious in composing words of blessing.
Preserve me from all evil tidings, and the terror they inspire,
And from whatever frightful events that might befall.

My Lady Mary—
Gentle Dove, like a hen that shelters her chickens,[21]
Protect me under the wings of your compassion,
From the snatching talons of the evil hawk[22]

Ethiopian singer takes the Dove as a liturgical processional item for the celebration
of God's victory (cf. Ps 68.24–26). Mary is again seen as the fulfilment of the type of
the Elect Israel favored by God.
     [20]Song 2.14.
     [21]Cf. Mt 23.37.
     [22]Ps 74.19.

That makes me fear for my life.
When I rise in the morning, I offer you my prayers:
May the radiance of your face light up the darkness of my mind.
The force of my love for you wakens my heart from sluggish sleep.
Hear the voice of my prayer and grant me your favor.

In the name of God the Father, who anointed you
   With the oil of sanctity and purity,[1]
   And in the name of God the Son, who was formed in your womb,
   And in the name of the God the Holy Spirit, who overshadowed
      you,[2]
   So do I salute you, My Lady Mary, raising my voice,
   To speak out what has been hidden from ages past;[3]
   Those symbolic types of you that have been manifested and
      proclaimed.

BLESSED Virgin, Elected One,
We name you a Paradise in which the perfumed tree is planted.[4]
We name you the Fountain, from which gushes forth the water of
   life.[5]
We name you the Land, which bore the apple fruit.
We name you the Bush which was enwrapped in fire.[6]
We name you the Rod which budded forth a shoot.[7]
We name you the Pole which bore the cluster of grapes.[8]
We name you the Fleece which was covered in dew.[9]
We name you the Tent of Dwelling, covered in glory.[10]
We name you the Ark, covered with the Mercy-Seat.[11]
We name you the Cloud which rained down food.[12]

[1] Cf. Ps 45.7.
[2] Lk 1.35.
[3] Cf. Book of Enoch 24.4f.
[4] Gen 2.9; Rev 2.7.
[5] Song 4.15.
[6] Ex 3.2f.
[7] Num 17.2f.
[8] Num 13.24.
[9] Judg 6.36f. God gave Gideon the sign of the fleece covered with dew as a confirmation that he would deliver Israel from its enemies.
[10] Ex 40.34–36.
[11] Ex 25.17–21.
[12] Ps 78.27–28.

We name you the Dove, whose sides were covered with red hued
    gold.[13]
We name you the Turtle Dove whose wings stretch over her
    chickens.[14]
We name you the Ship laden with riches.[15]
We name you the Harbor, that calms the heaving sea.
We name you the Land that gives a rich crop.
We name you a Heaven . . .[16]
. . .[17] and the Cherubim bear you up.
O Virgin, your glory is deeper than the Abyss, and higher than the
    heavenly heights;
There is no human tongue which can exhaust your praise.
Now I pray to you with fervent request, incomparable Queen,
Protect me in your majesty; grant to me your clemency.
Gentle Lady, to whom revenge is wholly foreign,
Gird me about with your righteousness and endow me with
    courage.
My spirit calls upon you; in you my heart has put its trust.
May your mercy follow me all the days of my life.[18]

My Lady Mary—
Mother of the Lord of All,
He who was before the world and shall be to the ages of ages,
Like the Olive, you are a tree of sweet smelling balsam.
Your tears of pity, like rain on our deserts, render all our bitterness
    sweet.
Through you the sick are healed and the wounded regain strength.

[13]Ps 68.13–14.
[14]Cf. Deut 32.11; Lk 13.34.
[15]Prov 31.14.
[16]Two half lines are missing in the Ms. Byzantine hymnology would typically
add here "who contained Him the heavens could not contain" (the *Platytera* title of
the Virgin).
[17]Probably: "We name you the Throne". The Throne is another aspect of the
Platytera title, as Mary's womb is a "throne greater than the heavens."
[18]Ps 23.6.

Through you kings have their dominion,[19] and princes act bravely.
Through you the weary are fortified, and the humble are exalted.[20]
Through you the wretched come into honor, and the poor are
 made rich.[21]
Those who place their trust in you shall never be condemned, nor
 shall they perish.
O Virgin, you are the Gushing Spring of the Fount of Wisdom;
Water me with the torrent of the Gospel of your Son,
And protect me by his Cross.
Cover me with his mercy; gain for me his compassion;
Strengthen me by his anointing; restore me with his apples;[22]
Lead me into your vineyard's cellar that I might be with you
 there.[23]
Establish in me, as from your Son, a love that is most noble.

My Lady Mary—
Mother of the Mighty God,
Earth honors you; the heavens exalt you.
You are veiled in the Court of Glory;
The wings of Cherubim cover you.[24]
You are the Perfect Tabernacle of which Paul spoke,[25]
Sprinkled with divine blood,
Unlike the Tabernacle of Eli at Shiloh, asperged with the blood of
 goats and bulls.[26]

---

[19]Prov 8.15. An attribute of Sophia in the Scriptural text. The poet goes on to show the relation between Sophia–Logos and the Mother of the Incarnate Lord. She is the "gushing forth" of waters from the Spring of Wisdom (the Logos) which historically she bore in the Incarnation.

[20]Cf. Lk 1.48, 52.

[21]Lk 1.53.

[22]Song 2.5.

[23]Song 2.4: like the Lover and his Beloved.

[24]Once again Mary is depicted as the Ark of the Covenant, shrine of the divine presence (the Logos).

[25]Heb 9.11.

[26]1 Sam 1.

You are the Ark which David, that friend of Barzillai's,[27] celebrated
    with songs
When it came back from the land of the Philistines.[28]
Holy Lady, clad in purity and crowned with sanctity,
When I am glad of heart I shall sing the glory of your name.
When I am sad, then I shall pour out my prayers before you.
For your part, pray for me to your Son
That he might free me from the hands of evil men,
And from the teeth of deadly beasts;
From the lips of false calumniators, and from all lying tongues.[29]

My Lady Mary—
Fiery Chariot of the Godhead[30]
More splendid than the Sun, and more radiant than the Moon,[31]
Bride from the Land of Galilee[32]
What shall I call you?[33] To what graceful thing shall I compare
    you?
Shall I liken you to the rosy skin of the ripened apple?[34] Or to the
    lily in flower?[35]

---

[27] 2 Sam 19.32–40. Barzillai the Gileadite was a faithful friend of David, an old
man, who dreamed of seeing his ancestral home once more after he had crossed the
Jordan. He becomes a type of the wise disciple longing for heavenly salvation. Perhaps
the idea has a strong resonance with the poet.

[28] 2 Sam 6.

[29] Ps 120.2.

[30] The Shekinah or cloud containing the Glory of God. It was the Shekinah which
translated Elijah to heaven in the form of a fiery chariot (cf. 2 Kg 2.11–12). Mary, who
gives birth to the Word, is considered mystically under this title.

[31] Rev 12.1.

[32] Cf. Song 4. 8. The titles of Song 4.12, following, are standard mariological epi-
thets in Byzantine hymnology.

[33] The phrase is from the Byzantine Hymn to Mary (the *Theotokion*) found at the
end of the Office of Compline. It is set on the lips of the Angel of Annunciation: "Awed
by the beauty of your virginity, and the immense radiance of your purity, Gabriel
called out to you, Theotokos: What fitting hymn of praise can I offer you? And what
shall I call you? I stand confused and in awe, and so, as commanded, I cry out to you:
Rejoice, Full of Grace."

[34] Song 4.3, 6.7.

[35] Song 2.2.

Shall I name you the Golden Omer?[36] Or the fountain of living
    water?[37]
Shall I name you Branch of the Vine, heady with the fruit of grape?
Perhaps I should name you that Field in which no thorn or thistle
    can grow?[38]
Or the Tree of Life, which God's right hand has planted,[39]
Whose fruit shall never wither, whose foliage shall not fade?[40]
O City full of treasure, O Land of all wealth,
Establish a covenant with me, by swearing a bond:
Hide me from the power of death, which seizes us like the wild
    dog.
Lead me, like Enoch the father of Methuselah, into the land of the
    living.
Allow me to be there rejoicing.

My Lady Mary—
Sacred Ark of the Tablets of the Commandments,
Shaded by the covering wings of the Cherubim,
The princes of Syria and Cilicia brought precious woods to adorn
    your house.[41]
O Virgin, horn of royal unction,[42] crystal vessel of priestly
    anointment,
The gate of your flesh is sealed, closed with the lock of virginity.
Accept my prayer as if it were a libation of wine and other gifts[43]

---

[36]The measurement of Manna which Moses commanded should be placed in the Ark of the Covenant alongside the tables of commandments. The poet envisages the Omer as a golden jar of Manna. Mary is the receptacle of the (Eucharistic) body of the Lord.

[37]Song 4.15.

[38]Is 7.23f.

[39]Cf. Ps 79.15–16. The poet combines the images of the Tree of Life (Gen 2.9) with the "Vine the Lord's right hand has planted," as a synthetic image of Mary.

[40]Cf. Enoch cc. 24–25.

[41]Cf. 1 Kg 5.6–10.

[42]1 Kg 1.39.

[43]Cf. Num 15.4–5.

And enable it to rise up on my behalf into the heavenly court of
     your Son.
As for those who seek after my soul,
Let them be brought to sackcloth and garments of mourning.[44]
May the hour of distress fall upon them, and bring them to a day
     of calamity.
May the people shake their heads over them so that they become a
     byword among the gentiles.[45]

My Lady Mary—
Mother of the Most High God,
You are greater than the Cherubim and more glorious than the
     Seraphim.
You are the burnished throne of glory; the flaming chariot of fire,
On which the Ancient of Days was enthroned,
Which Daniel, that prince of divination,[46] contemplated in his
     dream.[47]
O Virgin, you are a Cloud, and your Son is a Treasury of mercy;
You a Treasury yourself, and your Son is a chest of riches.
You are the stem of the vine, and your Son is the grape.
O Daughter of David, you are the Bride of the King of Israel.
I cry out before you as a suppliant. I make my prayer before your
     face:
Console me, a wanderer, who am so oppressed by sadness.
Give me the fullness of joy, a joy that will never decay,
And make me flourish all my days.

O Lady Mary—
Dove of Virginity,
I shall praise you gloriously, and extol you with blessings,

[44]Cf. Is 22.12.
[45]Ps 43.15.
[46]Dan 4.6.
[47]Dan 7.9–10.

For you are the mother of Him who existed before the ages.
In the narrow space of your womb you carried Him
Whom the space of heaven is not sufficient to contain,
Him whom the expanse of earth cannot enfold,
And you supported all his power.
No Tabernacle of Shiloh are you;[48] Indeed you are the Tabernacle of Justice,
Wherein they shall drink no intoxicating wine.[49]
You are the Vessel of First-Fruits[50] of the grape,
The Basket of the First-Fruits of the wheat harvest;
You are the Sacred Diadem which was given to Joshua for his coronation,[51]
When God ended the captivity of Jacob, and showed him his favor.[52]
My Queen, everything falls short of your loveliness;
There is nothing that is comparable to your beauty.
The Moon in all its fullness is not more lovely than you.
The sun in the height of its glory cannot outshine you.
As a suppliant I bend down before you and pray:
Illumine my heart, which is as black as soot,
And once more, as from a raging storm, deliver my soul from despondency.

[48] 1 Kg 1.3.
[49] Cf. 1 Kg 1.13–14.
[50] Deut 26.2.
[51] Zech 6.11; Joshua or "Jesus the Priest" was a patristic symbol of Christ.
[52] Ps 125.1–7.

In the name of God the Father who spread his favor over you;
  And in the name of God the Son, who was clothed in your flesh;
  And in the name of God the Holy Spirit, who cast his shadow over
    you;[1]

So shall I sing to you, my Lady Mary, a song of mercy and justice,
For as I sing so shall I understand the way of innocence.[2]

*C*OME, for I shall liken you to the cup in which was poured the
    miraculous water.[3]

I shall compare you to the table covered in red gold.[4]

I shall compare you to the chalice brimming with unmixed wine.[5]

I shall compare you to the altar that bore the incense.[6]

I shall compare you to the wedding, for which the feast was made
    ready.[7]

O Virgin, you are the boast of Adam and Eve,

Because of you, the locked gate of Paradise has been re-opened.[8]

Because of you, the way of life has been made smooth once more.

O Pure One, through your purity, cleanse the defiled temple of my
    body.

You whose name is so sweet, salt with the flavor of your love, these
    insipid lips of mine.

Fountain of Glory, set me as a bucket dropped in your holy stream,
    that overflowing river of joy.

My Lady Mary—

[1]Lk 1.35.
[2]Ps 100.1–2.
[3]Judg 6.38.
[4]Ex 25.23.
[5]Cf. Ps 74.9.
[6]Ex. 37.25.
[7]Mt 22.1–2.
[8]Gen 3.25.

Hyacinthine vestment which was the noble robe of the King of
    Israel,
You are the Holy of Holies, that place reserved for the High Priest
    alone.[9]
You are the Golden Ladle that drew out the libation of wine.[10]
You are the Washbowl wherein the unclean are purified.[11]
O Blessed One, I pray to you: watch over me every single day.
Let them be overcome with shame and disgrace,
All those who rejoice over my sufferings,[12]
Who open wide their mouths against me in boasts.[13]

My Lady Mary—
Draped in the garment of clemency,
And clothed in the raiment of mercy,
I greet you with the salutation: Hail![14]
Accept my greeting of peace, and grant prosperity to all my paths.
Dig out from my members the root of transgression and sin.
Wash away the filth of my soul in blood from the side of your Son,
And clothe my limbs in the royal purple of holiness and purity.
Stretch out your wings, always to overshadow and protect me.[15]
Whenever I call upon you, come to my assistance.

My Lady Mary—
Splendor of Prophecy, Fountain of Joy,
The heavens of the heavens bow down before you.
Earth proclaims you as its foundation.
The depths sing your praises,

[9]Lev 16.17.
[10]Ex 25.29.
[11]Ex 30.17.
[12]Ps 70.13.
[13]Cf. Ps 34.21.
[14]Lk 1.28. The phrase also evokes the Byzantine rite of the *Chairetismoi* ("The Sayings of the All-Hail") which was based on the great Akathist poem reciting Mary's titles as if from the mouth of the Angel of the Annunciation.
[15]Cf. Ps 90.4.

And when a song is raised for you,
The rivers stretch out their hands.[16]
O Virgin, may my lips ever sound the praises of your name,
For no tarnish of sin or impurity ever marred the temple of your
    body.
May my heart be ever fixed on serving you.
Most Beautiful of Guides, the glory of my life,
Bear me safely on the path of salvation, from this world to the
    next.
As for those who hate my soul: smash them like a potter's jar.[17]

My Lady Mary—
Daughter of the priest Joiada[18]
Opening that gives into the Place of Mystery[19] not made by human
    hand,
Graced with all holiness, and praised in song,
O Virgin, show your radiant face to me.[20]
Let me hear the delightful sound of your voice.
May the lamp of your peace be my guide along the path.[21]

My Lady Mary—
Graced in holiness and purity,
Beautiful Bride, as lovely as the dawn,[22]
Shining more brightly than the Sun,
More radiant than the Morning Star,

[16]Cf. Ps 97.8.

[17]Ps 2.9.

[18]2 Kg 11.1–12. Joiada was the priest who restored the Davidic line of descent, and brought forth the true King-Messiah for the people of Israel.

[19]Ezek 40.7, according to the Ethiopic text. Mary is like the vision of the divine Temple given to Ezekiel. She contains the inner sanctum of the presence of God, the divine Word in her womb.

[20]Song 2.14.

[21]Ps 118.105.

[22]Song 6.9.

Chosen Lady, you came forth from a noble stock, from a glorious
    people.
O Virgin, Bridal Chamber that contained all Wisdom,
As often as I stretch out my hands to you as suppliant,
Accept my prayer, as if it were the perfume of burning incense.[23]
Grant that I may ever be protected by the covering of your grace,
Clothed in the mantle of your clemency,
Freed from the chains of my sins,
Saved from every snare of the Maleficent.

My Lady Mary—
You are the golden cup that brings joy,
The silver basin, the washbowl of purifying water.
You are the workshop of the Spirit,
The place where all profitable transaction occurs;
The place even of oblation, where incense is offered.
You are the golden wreath of the priestly tiara,[24]
The sacerdotal vestment that was to be worn.[25]
I offer this gift of benediction and praise in your name.
As often as I invoke you, in secret or aloud, so I pray you,
Come to me and save me. Be near me and set me free.

---

[23]Ps 140.2; Rev 8.3–4.
[24]Cf. Ex 39.30–31.
[25]Ex 28.31.

In the name of God the Father who created your body in holiness
    and purity,
  And in the name of God the Son, who made you his mother,
  And in the name of God the Holy Spirit, who spread his shadow
    over you,
  I shall sing your praise, my Lady Mary,
  All the while proclaiming your blessed and lovely memory,
  And recounting the wonders of your graciousness;
  For you have brought health to those who were far off,
  And peace to those who were near at hand.[1]

*D*EAREST Virgin—a heaven I name you, a celestial region.
A cloud I name you, bearing rain within.
A temple I name you; that sealed Eastern Gate.[2]
Most holy I name you; portico of the sanctuary.
A garden I name you, for from you was harvested the Grape of
    Life.
O Tower of defense, I have set you as my strong fortress of refuge,[3]
The pillar of my life: the Balaz of my faith, and the Yaqam of my
    action.[4]
I have made you my shade, a tree so beautiful to the eye[5]
Which brought forth so tender a branch.

[1]Eph 2.17. The Ephesians text applies the reconciliation to Christ, who effects
salvation "through his body." The poet here envisages Mary as the medium of that
reconciliation, as she is the provider of Christ's salvific body.

[2]Ezek 44.2. The eastern gate of the Temple was the one God himself entered in,
and for this reason it was "sealed." For patristic thought the sealed gate signified the
womb of Mary, who was both Virgin and Mother. In this patristic exegetical trope,
she was the "sealed gate" of the Temple, which contained the divine presence, and
through which the divine presence came into the material world in the incarnation
of the Logos.

[3]As in Ps 18.2.

[4]The Ethiopic bible designates the twin columns mentioned in 1 Kg 7.21 (Boaz
and Jachin) by these names. They were the towering twin pillars that framed the
entrance to the Temple of Solomon.

[5]Gen 3.6.

I have set you as the seal of my consummation,[6] and the
    consummation of my end.
I have set you as the staff in my right hand, and the rod in my left.
O Blessed One, because of you all distress has ceased,
And blessing has descended for one who had been accursed[7]
Because of you, error came to an end,
And the burden of sin was cast down into the depths of mercy.[8]
Because of you, sadness has been driven away,
And the sickness of sin has come to an end.
O Fountain of Glory who gush forth the sweet water of joy,
Give me to drink from the spring of your mercy,
And water me in my inmost heart.
Grant that I might be set at the right hand of your Son,
That day when all that has grown old is made young once more,
When all that has been asleep, is brought awake again.

My Lady Mary—
Mother of the Mystical Lamb
Who by the sprinkling of his blood, purified the sin of the whole
    world,[9]
You are that priestly horn of unction[10]
By which the kings of the earth are anointed
And with which the priests of the mysteries are signed.
You are the Outpouring of prophecy,
In which young men speak oracles, and old men dream dreams.[11]

---

[6]Rev 9.4. Those who did not bear the seal of God were subject to assault in the
last days of the consummation. Here the poet characterizes the Virgin Mary as the
protective seal of God, and invokes her assistance in the days of his own consummation—his death.

[7]The poet praises the Virgin's benediction of his own life, but also invokes her role
as Birth-Giver of God, through whom the curse of Adam over the entire human race
was lifted by the Incarnation of the Logos from the holy Theotokos.

[8]Cf. Mic 7.19.

[9]Jn 1.29; Heb 9.12–14, 20–28.

[10]Cf. 1 Sam 16.1; 1 Kg 1.39.

[11]Joel 3.1.

You are that Month of Peace in which the reapers rejoiced,
And the harvesters made merry.[12]
You are the Fortified City where the just live in safety
And rest from all their afflictions.[13]
You are the Seed of Justice, for the remnant of the House of
    Israel.[14]
You are the Beginning of Life and Salvation,[15]
The cause of boasting among your people.[16]

O Virgin, those who were renowned because of their greatness,[17]
Men of clemency, whose righteousness will never be forgotten,[18]
Raised up and constructed a wonderful monument to you,
Although they could never fully tell your praises.
O Chosen One, in the name of your Son, I beg you,
Do not shut me out from your ineffable wedding feast[19]
Which will endure without ending.
My Lady Mary—
You are the blessed tree, more lovely than all other trees,[20]
Which bears fruit in all seasons, bringing in a harvest every
    month,
Abounding in unfailing wealth of figs,
Never shaken by the rough winds of sin,
Never hurt by the pruning knives of transgression.

[12]Is 9.3.

[13]Cf. Ps 121.3–4; Is 26.1–3; Heb 11.16, 12.22; Rev 21.12–27.

[14]Is 6.13.

[15]As Mother of the Incarnate Word who brought life to the Cosmos.

[16]Jdt 15.10. "You are the glory of Jerusalem, the proud boast of Israel. You are the highest honor of our race." These acclamations are commonly transferred to the Theotokos in the Byzantine hymnic tradition.

[17]Sir 44.3.

[18]Sir 44.10–15.

[19]Lk 14.24; Mt. 25.11–13.

[20]The poet's imagery of trees turns around the fruitful fig, but also alludes here, as in the following verses, to the notion of the Tree of Jesse, and the Tree of Life. As Jesus is the true Vine, the poet considers Mary as the Vine stock, the "rod of Jesse," from which the King was to come.

You are the Pavilion of Light, whom no tent maker has ever
fashioned.
You are the Temple of Heaven,[21] not the earthly temple of
Benjamin.[22]
You are the Scepter of the Kingdom, from the root of Jesse,[23]
Not the scepter of Saul of the tribe of Shimeah.[24]
O Queen, who stand at the right hand of the King,[25]
Lay your sacred hands upon my head,
And hear the voice of my prayer.
Do not turn a deaf ear to my cries,
But guide the longing of my soul, and grant my heart's deep prayer.

My Lady Mary—
You are the Vine of Justice, not the vineyard of Sibmah,[26]
Chosen from all the trees of the world.
By the blood of the grape you bore, all the curse of Eve was lifted.
By your seal, the gate of Paradise was unlocked and laid open.
You are the mountain of prophecy which was named Ramatha[27]
On which the company of prophets gave forth their music,
Mystical teachings accompanied by song.[28]
You are that Ab'Enezer, whose name was changed to "Stone of
Assistance"[29]

[21]Cf. Rev 11.19.

[22]The Temple at Shiloh.

[23]Is 11.1.

[24]Whose lineage was rejected in favor of that of David (of the House of Jesse):
see 1 Chr 8.32.

[25]Ps 44.10.

[26]Which the gentiles desolated: see Is 16.8.

[27]1 Kg 19.18–19. It was the home of the brotherhood of prophets with Samuel.

[28]Some Ethiopian clergy were also skilled on the lyre, and saw in this liturgical
task a mimesis of the priests of the ancient temple (the Psalmists and Levites). The line
is an indication that this poem was probably originally performed as a priestly (and
prophetic) courtly song to the accompaniment of the lyre. The association, here, with
the "brotherhood of prophets" suggests the manner in which the monks of Ethiopia
saw in their vocation a direct continuation of prophetic charism in the church, under
the aegis of the Theotokos.

[29]1 Sam 7.12.

Which in the time of the Old Covenant,
The priest Samuel[30] set up as a memorial.
You are the spring of running water,[31]
Which you caused to spring up, and give light to Sion.
You are . . .[32]
When he killed the two dragons in the land of Susa.[33]
O Bride, crowned with grace and majesty,
From the table of justice, nourish me in the portico of your temple.
Grant to me an earthly habitation where no troubles or problems
        disturb me.

My Lady Mary—
You are the flower of cinnamon and balsam
Hand-chosen by the importer of perfumes.
You are what Paul, the priest of Rome, called the perfect
        tabernacle,[34]
In whom dwelt the High Priest of Heaven himself.
You are the glorious Cloud of Life,
The rain cloud that carries the dew of clemency.
Your praiseworthiness far exceeds all bounds, and all our capacity,
For the praises of your loveliness will be ceaseless and unending.
The mystery of your greatness surpasses speech or explanation;
The measure of your glory cannot be assessed by silver or gold.

[30]Cf. 1 Sam7.9.

[31]Cf. Ps 64.2, 10.

[32]Lost manuscript line relating to a typology from the Book of Daniel which is cited in the next line. It might well be a reference to the Virgin as the "Bait" (Dan 14.26) which, when he had consumed it, destroyed the Dragon. In Patristic literature (especially visible in Gregory of Nyssa's *Catechetical Oration*), the motif of Christ being the "bait" which Satan takes (destroying the body of Jesus on the cross) like some great sea beast, only to find it has been hooked and caught, is a favored theme for depicting the power of the saving incarnation.

[33]A reference to the story of Bel and the Dragon in Dan 14.

[34]Heb 9.11.

O Mother, nourish me on justice, and guard me in peace
As once you did for James the Brother[35]
When you found him orphaned, deprived of his own mother.
I ask life of you, grant my prayer,[36]
Do not let me be carried away in the midst of my allotted span.[37]
But free me from the shackles of sin,
Take off my chains of guilt that cause such sorrow.

My Lady Mary—
Hall of sanctification, most exalted sister,
Whom the army of spirits, those burning embers,[38] longed to gaze
    upon.[39]
You are the vestment of faith, that garment woven of many colors[40]
Over which were worn the Gems of Remembrance,[41]
Jewels made from onyx stones[42] and carved like the gems of a
    signet.[43]
O Virgin, you were the zeal of Reuben when he tried to flee from
    the curse of death.[44]
You were the champion of the battalions of Simeon and Levi
When they assailed the land of Sichem.[45]
You are the riches of the princely state of Judah,
That whelp of the fearsome lion;[46]

[35]James, "the Brother of the Lord," was traditionally regarded in Ethiopia as the adopted brother of Jesus.

[36]An echo of Ps 20.5.

[37]Is 38.10.

[38]The Seraphim, conceived as burning flames attending the throne of God.

[39]1 Pet 1.12.

[40]The high-priestly garment, Ex 28.6f.

[41]Ex 28.12. The gems were part of the High Priest's prophetic role and were used in ancient times in the oracular rites of the Temple.

[42]Ex 28.9.

[43]Ex 28.11.

[44]The story is narrated in the Apocryphal *Testament of the 12 Patriarchs* (Reuben 1. 9–10).

[45]Gen 49.7.

[46]Gen 49.9.

The inheritance of the tranquil Issachar[47]
Who was the reward for the field of mandrakes.[48]
You are the gate of the dwelling of Zabulon,[49]
The sweet-smelling palm of Napthali,
The oil on the feet of Asher.[50]
You are the abundance of grace Joseph enjoyed in the land of Ham,
The fullness of the blessing of Gad,[51]
The fortress of the land of Benjamin,[52]
The host of Manasseh's thousands, and the gift of the blessing of
    Ephraim.[53]
O Virgin, your praises can never be properly told,
Neither by the lips of men, nor by the tongues of the spirits whose
    cry is unending,
For wherever the divine dominion of your glorious Firstborn holds
    sway
There too is proclaimed your wondrous exaltation.
O Blessed Lady who bring the gift of peace,
Bless me with the blessing of father and mother.
Snatch me from the grasp of those who work evil,
And save me from the hands of bloodthirsty men.[54]

My Lady Mary—
More fragrant than cinnamon, your memory is sweeter than
    balsam.[55]
He who shut the abyss with his seal, and fastened up the frightful
    place,[56]

[47]Gen 49.15.
[48]Gen 30.14.
[49]Gen 49.13.
[50]Deut 33.24.
[51]Deut 33.20.
[52]Deut 33.12.
[53]Deut 33.17.
[54]Ps 58.3.
[55]Ezek 27.19, according to the Ethiopic text
[56]Rev 20.3.

Was carried in your womb, and you became his mother.
He who set in place the dry land upon the waters
And built the heavens, making a roof for the winds,
Called you his sanctuary and made you his own heaven;[57]
None other than He who gathered the waters of the sea as if in a
    bag
And poured them into the containers of the deep places.[58]
O Virgin, no one can fully recite your praises
Or explain them in words or books.
Elect Lady, I ask you earnestly,
Save me from the traps which yawn open against me
To swallow and devour me.[59]
Lift me from the tumult of the waters[60] which rise to drown me
And snatch me from the teeth of wild beasts,
That go around roaring for their prey,[61] doing all manner of evil.
Cover me with the mercy of your Son
And give me his peace as my adornment.

---

[57] A reference to the Byzantine tradition of Mary *Platytera* ("She who is wider than the heavens"); for as the heavens were unable to contain the deity, her womb nevertheless contained him, showing herself to be *Platytera*.

[58] Ps 32.7.

[59] Ps 68.16.

[60] Ps 123.4–5.

[61] Ps 103.21; 1 Pet 5.8.

In the name of God the Father who through his deity
  Elevated your flesh to regal dignity,
  And in the name of God the Son, who by his incarnation from you
  Was made King over the House of Jacob,
  And in the name of God the Holy Spirit, who purified and
    sanctified you
  That you might give birth to the King,
  I praise you My Lady Mary, that golden vessel[1] that carried the
    bread
  That more than satisfies the hunger of the starving.

ℰACH morning may my feet hasten in spirit,
To the house of your love, O Mother,
As I ever seek a full portion of your benediction.
Do not harden your heart towards me,
Nor turn away from me the lifting up of your face.[2]

My Lady Mary—
Decorated palace, from whose inner court there flowed the river
  of life,[3]
Blessed are all those who come each dawn of day
To your sacred threshold, seeking after your face.[4]
Blessed are they who run in the paths of your love[5]
And do not fall away from the ways of your law.[6]
For they shall be granted a seat to recline at your wedding feast
And share in the dominion of your Son.

[1] 1 Chr 28.16.
[2] Ps 99.2.
[3] Ezra 47.1f.
[4] Ps 26.8.
[5] Song 1.3.
[6] Ps 118.51.

My Lady Mary—
Mother of the honorable King,
Who offered a resplendent city
To whoever could profit with the talent,[7]
With yearning in my heart I pray to you:
Seek out most carefully the lost coin of my life.[8]
Do not permit my mind to wander along the byways of sloth and
    indolence,
For early in the morning I come to seek your blessing.

My Lady Mary—
You are our net, a safe place in the waves of this world
Where you gather the faithful of both sexes, like little fish,
Whenever they seek your help, or ask for that peace which you can
    grant.
See how, in a spiritual manner, I hasten my steps towards you.
Grant O Virgin, that my feet may wholly turn back
From the paths of wickedness.

My Lady Mary—
Queen who gave birth to the King
In manner so mystical that transcends our mind and imagination.
Zealously I seek the nuptial chamber of your love,
Make me turn back from the ways of sin
And grant me peace of soul, and chastity of heart.

My Lady Mary—
Mother of the Great King
Whom the Father begot from his own bosom before the ages,
Blessed is he who knocks on the gate of your palace[9]
And who comes at dawn to your hallways,[10]

---

[7]Lk 19.19.
[8]Lk 15.8–9.
[9]Prov 8.34.
[10]Alluding to Prov 8.17 (LXX).

Seeking from you the prize of a good recompense.
Blessed is he who keeps the way of your commandments[11]
And who proves himself an initiate of your Son's teaching.
Under your shade will he rest,
And in the nuptial chamber of your house will he be received.

My Lady Mary—
What knowledge bedecks you, what chastity crowns you!
Just as sin once brought the Kingdom of Death to power,[12]
So your grace makes the Kingdom of Justice spring forth.
Just as the Sunrise dispels the shadows of the dawn,
So too the light of faith in your Son dispels the darkness of sin.
Blessed is he who seeks after your love,
Whose footsteps tread the threshold of your house at break of
     day;[13]
Such a man will be satisfied with your blessing, filled to abundance.

[11]Prov 6.32.
[12]Rom 5.21.
[13]Cf. Sir 6.36.

In the name of God the Father who loved your beauty,[1]
   And in the name of God the Son who dwelt within your womb,
   And in the name of God the Holy Spirit
   Who was pleased to spread his shadow over you,
   I bless you, my Lady Mary, all the day long,
   And I shall tell of your wonderful greatness.
   All forms of beauty that exist were made for the sake of you,
   The appearances of all that is, were made with reference to the
      wonder that is you.
   From the beginning you were remembered in the Scroll of the
      Book,[2]
   Above all the wonderful things of this world your beauty causes
      wonderment.

F OR you, O Virgin, are like that seed which produced the
      harvest,[3]
You are like the heavens, which cause the day to break.
You are like the earth, which flows with milk and honey.[4]
You are like a garden[5] glorious in flowers and delightful fruits.
You are like the Holy of Holies, sheltered by the wings of the
      Cherubim.[6]
You are like the Ark, which bore within it the Tablets of the
      Covenant.
You are like that ship which gathered in riches beyond imagining.[7]
O Virgin, angels and humans are gathered in one assembly.[8]

[1]Ps 44.12.
[2]LXX Ps 39.8–9; also cf. Gen 1.26–27 (the book which is the "scroll" of all the scriptures).
[3]Mt 13.8, 24.
[4]Ex 13.5.
[5]Song 4.12.
[6]Ex 25.20.
[7]Prov 31.14.
[8]The common praise of the Virgin ("More honorable than the Cherubim . . .") forms the liturgical unity of the angelic choir and that of the church praying on earth.

Through you the world is liberated from slavery,
And because of you the Prince of Darkness was brought to
      nothing.
Through you the world is called to salvation,
And because of you war has been banished to the ends of the
      earth.[9]
Elect Lady, I beseech you earnestly
That you would make of me a worthy heart
Deigning to keep me in mind, and remembering me in your
      intercession.[10]

My Lady Mary—
You are the throne of the God of heaven,
Which the four-faced animals held up.[11]
The powers of heaven,
Made by the breath of the mouth of your Son,
Fall down prostrate before you, singing psalmody to you.
You they obey and you they serve.
The prophets praise you, who from long times before had
      contemplated you.[12]
The Apostles celebrate you, who were the teachers of the Kingdom
      of Heaven.
The Righteous bless you, who in patient endurance undertake
      asceticism.
The Martyrs honor you, all those who fought in the arena of their
      martyr's struggle.

O Queen who bore the King of Kings.
It is through you that kings enjoy their dominion[13]

---

[9]Cf. Ps 45.9–10.
[10]In the Blessed Virgin's eschatological intercession with Christ, on behalf of
the Church.
[11]Ezek 1.6f.
[12]Cf. Heb 11.13.
[13]A note relevant for an Ethiopian court-theologian to make!

And through you that princes obtain their honor.
Through you the humble are exalted,[14]
And those who have hatred in their heart are turned back to love.
The rich rejoice in you,
And the poor also spend their lives in hope because of you.
Good Lady, those who walk the earth, as well as those that fly in
the heavens,
Tell among themselves how it was that you found their salvation
for them,
And speak of the peace your mediation won for them.

O Pure One, fleece of living dew,[15]
Even though my sins are crimson red
They shall be made as white as snow.[16]
No trace of them will be able to be found.
For even if a host of my soul's enemies
Conspire to work a deadly evil against me
Your aid will scatter all their assembly.

My Lady Mary—
Daughter of Kohath and Merari,[17]
Daughter of Eliud[18] and daughter of Neri,[19]
You are the Vine of Righteousness
Bearing the Grape of Life
Which loosed the guilt of our sins
And gained for us indulgence.
O Elect Lady, Mother of the King of Mercy,
In you the freeman rejoices in his honor
And in you the homesteader is made rich.

[14]Lk 1.52.
[15]Judg 6.37.
[16]Is 1.18.
[17]Ex 6.16.
[18]Mt 1.14.
[19]Lk 3.27.

In you the hired man perseveres,
And in you the household slave is made free.
Merciful Lady, you are the mooring rope
Of mercy that never wears out.
Your right hand causes mercy and justice to play over me.
Good Lady, who never overlook anyone who is cast down,
Look upon me, your poor servant, with eyes of mercy.
Blessed Lady, who never turn away any suppliant,
May it please you to grant me salvation.
You who are the giver of good things, without reproach,[20]
Never inflicting harm on any soul,
Never let me be confounded in the hope I have placed in you.

My Lady Mary—
Beautiful jewel of the diadem,[21]
Which the great King of Israel himself placed on his brow,
You are the garland of gold, decorated with the engraving of
     sanctity[22]
With which the High Priest was crowned in the Temple of the
     Law.[23]
You are the vestment of the Memorial of Judgment[24]
Whose borders were made of skillfully woven work.[25]
With two twisted rings of gold on both its edges.[26]
You are the fabric of the Temple which Solomon built[27]
From mighty stones that were never hewn,[28]
Whose walls he lined with wood, and furnished with cedar
     planking,

[20]Jas 1.5.
[21]Is 62.3; Wis 18.24; Sir 47.6; Bar 5. 2–3.
[22]Sir 45.12.
[23]Ex 39.29.
[24]Ex 28.15.
[25]Ex 28.8.
[26]Ex 28.22–24. From the rings were hung the sacred high-priestly Ephod.
[27]1 Kg 6.1f.
[28]A symbol of the virginity of the Theotokos.

Covering both roof and pavements with gold.[29]
You are the Ark of the Covenant
Which brought blessing to the house of Amidara,
When he welcomed it hospitably in its time of wandering.[30]
O Virgin, honey from the comb of clemency,
Basin of the water of gentleness,
Make me into a harp and a lyre of the song of your praise.

My Lady Mary—
You are that sanctuary built by the Son of Were[31]
Crafted from gold and decorated with topaz,
Which had windows and a hall of meeting.
You are a garden
Where aromatic spices grow;
An altar wreathed in clouds of incense.
So shall I magnify your praise,
Singing psalmody for you
As once did Asaph, and Heman and the sons of Kore.[32]
Elect Lady, you travelled out of the people of Election,[33]
Clothe me with the purple of your purity
As if in the long robe of the priestly vesture,
And accept from my mouth this sacrifice,
As if it were a libation offered up in a sacred vessel.

My Lady Mary—
Daughter of the priest Eleazar[34]
Bride of the King, clad in vesture of glory and honor,[35]

[29]1 Kg 6.20–22.
[30]2 Sam 6.11, according to the Ethiopic text.
[31]Ex 31.2, according to the Ethiopic text.
[32]Psalmodists of the Old Testament.
[33]Like the Ark of the Covenant which left Israel and sojourned among the Philistines (1 Sam 5), so too the Theotokos came out of Israel and rested among the gentile Christians as their glory.
[34]Ex 6.23.
[35]Ps 44.14–15.

How delightful it is to hear you speak,[36]
For your voice is sweeter than honey,[37]
To be praised in the midst of the congregation.[38]
You are the House of Glory, in which dwelt the Lord of Angels;
You are the Mount of Horeb, a place of storms and darkness,
From which was heard the clamor of trumpets and the spoken
     word.[39]
You are the City of Wisdom, never looked on by the vulture's eye,
Through whose streets the lion and leopard[40] never prowl,
Where the steps of the proud have never trod.[41]

O Virgin, how sweet it is to remember you.
Humbly I celebrate you, on the lyre and with a psalm[42]
As once did Chonenias,[43] the head of the temple singers;
Or Asaph the psalmist;[44] or the sister of Moses on the shore of the
     sea;[45]
Or as Deborah once did on the summit of Tabor.[46]
Or Judith, in the presence of Achior,
When she had decapitated the Assyrian leader.[47]
Elect Lady, your praise overflows like water,
Cascading down the mountainside,
Running down to become a mighty sea.[48]
O Virgin, to praise you causes wonderment;
No one could rightly measure or estimate it properly.

[36]Song 2.14.
[37]Sir 24.20.
[38]Ps 21.23.
[39]Ex 19.16f.
[40]These animals are symbolic of evil in this instance.
[41]Cf. Job 28.7–8.
[42]Ps 97.5.
[43]1 Chr 15.27.
[44]1 Chr 6.39.
[45]Ex 20–21.
[46]Judg 5.1.
[47]Jdt 16: the Assyrian leader is Holofernes.
[48]Sir 24.23.

Your praise could never be spoken; of writing it there would be no
    end.
I pray to you, always and in every day,
Rescue me from unforeseen calamity, and from the noonday
    demon;
From the arrow that flies by day, and from the thing that walks in
    darkness.[49]

My Lady Mary—
You are Wisdom and Knowledge.
The Mighty God was well pleased in you[50]
And appointed you as his own little dwelling place,
Though no space on earth, nor even the fullness of the heavens,
Was ever wide enough to hold him.
You are the priestly vestment so splendid and magnificent:
Whose shoulders and frontal were so cleverly woven.
Just so, I place the seal of your love within my heart,
And wear your signet upon my arm as a sign.[51]
O giver of gifts in whom there is no contempt,[52]
Never allow me to be overcome in the battle, or to fall in the course
    of the race.
But intercede for me with your Son, and tell him this:
"Love this man, on my account, because he placed his trust in me;
And do not disappoint his trust; And even if he has sinned,
In your mercy forgive his transgressions."

[49]Ps 90.6.
[50]Cf. Mt 3.17.
[51]Song 8.6.
[52]Jas 1.5.

In the name of God the Father, who covered you with grace,
   And in the name of God the Son, who clothed himself in your
      flesh,
   And in the name of God the Holy Spirit, who sanctified you;

My Lady Mary—

GLADLY will I praise you with a new song,[1]
And bowing my head I venerate you.
Because of you, our ancestors recovered the Paradise of Delight
From which they had been cast out after eating the fruit of the
      forbidden tree.[2]
Because of you, the Man of Peace[3] was set free,
Even when the whole world was destroyed, and only eight souls
      survived.[4]
Because of you, Jacob was beloved, though the birthright of Esau
      was scorned.[5]
Because of you, David was chosen, and became the leader over
      Israel,
Gaining more honor than all his brothers,
And from Saul the Kingdom was taken and handed over to David.
O Pure Lady, create for me a chaste heart and an upright spirit.[6]

My Lady Mary—
Ark of the Temple of God,
Whom the Spirit overshadowed,[7] strengthening your right hand,
You are Joshua's column of witness,[8]

[1] Ps 32.3.
[2] Gen 3.23.
[3] Namely, Noah.
[4] Gen 7.13.
[5] Mal 1.2.
[6] Ps 50.12.
[7] Lk 1.35.
[8] Josh 24.26–27.

You are the strength that resided in the hair of Samson.[9]
You are the throne of Solomon,
Decorated with golden lions, six on each side.[10]
You are the bringer of peace to all who are in mutual strife,
The Purifier, for all who fall into sin.
The armies of the Seraphim celebrate you,
And the hosts of the Cherubim sing of your greatness.
Archangels fall down before you,
And the Powers of heaven shout out your holiness.
Royal Palace, Queen of the heavenly Spouse,
Grant that I may walk in your hallways
Where the elect recline,
Those who are clad in the wedding garment.[11]

My Lady Mary—
Like the Tree of Life of our first ancestors,[12]
You are ever-green, always renewed,
Never dried up or withered,[13]
More beautiful than the Cedar of Lebanon
And incomparably more lovely than the beauty of the field.[14]
O Queen, clad in gold, wearing the stole of majesty,
Spread your perfumed balsam liberally over my head,
Let me be drunk with the wine of your love,
The like of which no innkeeper could ever make.

My Lady Mary—
Ladder of Jacob,[15] whose summit reached the heavens;
Curtain of the Tabernacle, with the fifty clasps[16]

[9]Judg 16.17.
[10]1 Kg 10.20.
[11]Mt 22.11.
[12]Gen 2.9.
[13]Ps 1.3.
[14]Is 40.6; Mt 6.28–29.
[15]Gen 28.12.
[16]Ex 26.11.

On whose summit there rested the clouds of glory.[17]
You are Abisag,[18] the Nuptial Litter of the royal brother,[19]
Around which there stood sixty strong men of Israel.[20]
You are the Ark, the hiding place of men and beasts
At the time the dire waters flooded the earth.
You are the fulfillment of the prophecy of Daniel,[21] of the oracle
    about Susanna,[22]
For through you came justice and the remission of sins.[23]
O Virgin, whom the corruption of this age has never touched,
Cleanse me by your purity, from all the filth of worldly lusts.

My Lady Mary—
Outstanding in elegance and sanctity,
Signed with the seal of the Holy Trinity,
Shining as bright as the Sun, and as radiant as the Moon,[24]
You are the priestly staff of Aaron, the very Ark of the Mosaic Law,
The portion of Caleb's inheritance,[25]
And that of the riches of prince Joshua.[26]
You are the gift of blessing to the people of Ephraim and
    Manasseh.[27]
O Virgin, unknown by man, to you I offer this gift of praise
With a heart sincere and true.
O Queen, grant that I too may tread on the scorpion and dragon.[28]
Rescue me from ruin, and deliver me from destruction.

[17]The divine presence in the sanctuary: Ex 40.32, 36.

[18]1 Kg 1.3: "And the maiden was most beautiful."

[19]The Lover in the Song of Songs who calls his Bride "My Sister."

[20]Song 3.7.

[21]Dan 9.23f.

[22]Dan 13.31 (in the Vulgate): "For Susanna was delicate and fair beyond measure."

[23]Dan 9.24.

[24]Song 6.9.

[25]Josh 15.13.

[26]Who took possession of the Promised Land: Num 13.16.

[27]Deut 34.2.

[28]Ps 90.13.

My Lady Mary—
You are the Bush in the field of Horeb
Which put on fire as if it were a robe,[29]
Whose branches were not burned and whose foliage was not
     withered.[30]
You are the Garden[31] where vines and balsam flowers,
Where wild crocus and cinnamon, abound.
Or rather, you are the fruit-arbor of figs,
The orchard of pomegranates and olives.[32]
You are the mystical New Temple,[33]
Built of Sapphire and Agate.[34]
You are the Letter of Good Tidings
Which you made to be carried into the land of Persia
Borne by the flight of an eagle,
Taking the fruit of the medicinal tree
To console the heart of a people, who were living in direst need.[35]
O Virgin, crowned with majesty and grace,
The abyss of your glory is deeper far
Than the greatest depths of the ocean.
The sea of your praise is more profound than the great waters.
Neither tongue of men nor angels can tell it all,
Either with mighty voice, or in quiet speech.
O Pure One without flaw, Holy One without blemish,
Cleanse me that I might become pure.
Sanctify me and I shall be made holy.[36]
Strengthen me that I might not grow weary,
And guard me that I might not sin.

[29]Cf. Ps. 103.2.
[30]Ex 3.2f.
[31]Song 4.12–14.
[32]Num 13.23; Song 2.13.
[33]Rev 11.19.
[34]Rev 21.19.
[35]Reference to the Apocryphal Remnants of Baruch<B> 7.
[36]Jer 17.14.

My Lady Mary—
City of quiet and delight
In which the souls rest from their labors.[37]
You are the bean-seed carried to the sowing,
And the ingathering of vegetables, around which we sing at harvest
    time.
You are the strong Ark, protecting us from all tumult and disorder.
You are the one who at dawn brought the prince's army
To predestined victory over the people of Ai and Lachis.[38]
Bride whose lips are as ruby[39] as the peony,
Your refinements smell more sweetly than sherbet.
Fill me with your fragrance,
Which makes even the perfume of a garden seem poor in
    comparison.
Deliver me from the surge of the Sea of this Age; and be my safe
    harbor.

[37]Rev 14.13.
[38]Joshua, taking the Promised Land: Josh 7–10.
[39]Song 4.3.

*In the name of God the Father who marked you with such purity
    and righteousness;*

*And in the name of God the Son who took his origin from your
    womb;*

And in the name of God the Holy Spirit who made you his couch;

I come to you as a supplicant My Lady Mary, Turtle Dove,[1]

Whose wings were covered with the sheen of gold.[2]

I draw out your praises, and take up once more my hymn to you.

*H*ow Blessed you are O Virgin.
You are called the Tabernacle
That was not wholly enveloped.[3]
You are called the Ark, carrying the tablets of the Decalogue.
You are called the Humeral Vestment,[4] which bore the golden
    fastenings.
You are called the Mare.[5]
You are the Turban and Band of the crown engraved with
    holiness.[6]
You are called the Rod which sent forth branches.[7]
You are called the dish, which bore the warm bread for the
    sacrifices.[8]
You are called the Cloud, which bore the lightning flash.[9]
You are called the Tower and the Guarded House, the palace of the
    King.[10]

[1]Song 1.15; 2.10–14; 5.2; 6.9.

[2]Ps 67.13.

[3]Ex 36.14.

[4]The priestly Ephod which bore upon it the names of the Elect Tribes of Israel:
Ex 28.6–14.

[5]"Mare of Pharaoh's Chariots"–as a term of majesty and grace–Song 1.9.

[6]Ex 39.28–30.

[7]Num 17.8.

[8]Ex 25.29–30.

[9]Ex 19.16.

[10]Neh 3.25; Song 4.4; Tob. 13.16–18; 1 Chr 29.1.

You are called the Sanctuary,[11] which the angel measured with a
  rod of gold,
Finding it, after close measurement, six cubits on each side.[12]
You are called the Pitcher of milk, and the Wineskin of the vintage
  that brings joy.
You are called the Little Ship,
And also, the Harbor of safe anchorage.

O Virgin, in you the vision is made perfect,
The oracles of the prophets come true.
Through you God is made known in Judah,
And his name is great in Israel.[13]
Through the prophets the greatness of your kingdom was truly
  praised;
It has gone to the farthest reaches of the abyss,
And has been lifted above the heights of the heaven.
The fullness of your glory is deeper than the sea,
Endless, boundless, having no shore.
O Rod of faith, you became the support of the Son of Man.
Never let the grace of your help depart from me.
Never may the beast attack me, he that prowls on the sea shore.[14]
Do not allow me to become his plaything, or the mockery of his
  demons.
O Bride, do not permit me to spoil the nuptial garment of your
  banquet,
When my life ebbs away to its completion, and the time of death
  draws near.

[11]Rev 21.10–16: the Theotokos is the sanctuary of the New Jerusalem that has no
temple within it.
[12]Ezek 40.45: the walls of New Jerusalem are compared to the priestly Ephod in
Rev. 21 (where they are 144 cubits on all sides), and the Ethiopian hymn writer has
combined the ideas he found there, with the description of the Temple in Ezekiel. The
overriding image is that Mary is the holy sanctuary, who held within her the presence
of the Most High.
[13]Ps 75.2.
[14]The crocodile, symbol of the eschatological dragon: Rev 12.17.

My theme is a lofty one: I shall sing of the pomegranate juice of
    your love.[15]
Accept from me this mediocre fruit of my lips,[16]
Just as your Son found acceptable the pennies of the poor widow.[17]

My Lady Mary—
You are the Ark of Noah which remained after the flood
And which was his refuge and that of his sons.[18]
You were Abraham's seal, the mark of his righteousness,[19]
And the Field which he bought with his gold.[20]
You are the Gate of Dawn, through which rose the Sun of Justice,[21]
And his rays have warmed the whole creation.
When he came all radiance was manifested for the fulfillment of
    the commandments.
You are the Turning of Time,
The exact point of division between the Ages.
You are the Little Boat of Mercy, laden with all honorable treasures,
By which men can navigate the stormy sea of tribulations, lifted
    safe above the waves.
You are Hezekiah's poultice, made up from the fig tree
In the time when he was sick and near to death.[22]
O Bringer of Peace, you are the Reconciler of those who war
    among themselves,
The Vesture of Rejoicing, for those who were naked.
You are the safety of those who are near at hand,
And the crown of those who are far off.
O Bride, for those who put on the cloak of your mercy

[15]See Song 8.2.
[16]Heb 13.15.
[17]Lk 21.2.
[18]Gen 6.12f.
[19]Rom 4.1.
[20]Gen 23.4–20.
[21]Mal 4.2.
[22]Is 38.21.

And wear the torc of your love upon their necks,
Your goodness fills them to satiety[23] even to their old age.[24]
Elect Lady, whoever is made strong by the perfume of your name,
Or whoever gathers round for your sweet-smelling fruit,
Will find what they are seeking, and discover their heart's desire.
O Virgin of Salvation, whoever depends upon you, and is sustained
    by your assistance,
Will never be troubled by the rebellion of enemies,
Nor will they fall prey to unstable times.
You are the ample Wineskin of the vintage of rejoicing,
And when I moan like a dove,[25] or make mournful cry like a
    pelican,[26]
Whenever my tears drop to the ground, then console me;
Make me glad for the time when I knew grief.
Save me from my enemies when they open their mouths against
    me like traps.[27]

My Lady Mary—
Mother of the Divine Redeemer,
Suckled in purity, you grew up in sanctity,
You are the Bride of the King, wearing around your throat the
    necklace of mercy.
You are the Ladder of Intercession, carrying up to heaven the
    prayer of the saints.[28]
You are the Fountain of running streams[29] which waters the souls
    of the elect.
You are the vine-stock of the rich grape from the valley of
    Azekah.[30]

[23]Ps 103. 28.
[24]Ps 70.18.
[25]Is 38.14.
[26]Ps 101.7, according to the Ethiopic text.
[27]Ps 21.14.
[28]Cf. Rev 8.3–4.
[29]Song 4.15.
[30]Figuratively the Promised Land: Josh. 10.10.

You are the Sanctuary of God, which no earthly architect ever
    made,
And the closed East Gate of the Temple,[31] that no one ever opened
    or knocked at.
You are the Pouch of the Pearl which the thief could not find.
You are the beautiful chamber of the wedding banquet,
Offering a place to recline to all who have been invited to the
    wedding of your Son.
Radiant One, let the splendor of your kindness graciously dawn
    upon me.

You the Just One who makes sinners just,
Make peace for me, and reconcile me with your Son.
O Strong Staff that holds up the waverer,
Do not depart from me by day or night:
Watch over and guard me, be ever ready to protect me.
Save me from my enemies, who gnash their teeth against me,[32]
And from the deceitful man who mixes poisons and spells.

My Lady Mary—
Daughter of Isaac who was married to Rebecca,
Daughter of Abijah, son of Ma'acah.[33]
You are the abundant dowry of Leah,[34] and the gift of blessing over
    her children.
You are the Rod on which Moses leaned, which divided the Red
    Sea,[35]
When Egypt perished in the midst of the Month of Nisan.[36]
You are the mystical sanctuary,

[31]Ezek 44.1–3.
[32]Ps 34.16.
[33]2 Chr 11.22.
[34]Gen 30.20.
[35]Ex 14.16.
[36]April—hence Passover time.

Which was wrapped in storm cloud and the darkness of thunder.[37]
You are the Untouchable Ark,
Containing the tablets of the commandments,
Before which the god Dagon fell prostrate
And was in pieces before the threshold.[38]
You are the priestly tunic[39] woven of many colors, by Belseel the
    weaver
Which was joined at its sides by two shoulder-pieces.[40]
O Beautiful One, You are the Turtle Dove in the field of Heaven,
To you who sit at your Son's right hand,
I pray from the very depth of my heart;
Grant my heart's desire, and the prayers of my inmost soul.
Turn to hear my prayer, and give it back to me like a precious gem.
May my prayers come before you like a flying arrow, sent up into
    the ether,
And may they not return to me, empty and void.

My Lady Mary—
Tabernacle of Saul,[41] that teacher of the Greeks,
Whom the princes of Cilicia and Phoenicia held in esteem,
You are that Arbor which is called the Choice Vine[42]
And the Cloud of Grace that shone over the land of Falel and
    Maacah.[43]
You are the Meadow to which the flock is driven through the
    Sheep Gate.[44]
You are the strength of true faith which was found in Eunice.[45]
O Dove, whom the hawk can never overcome,

[37] Ex 40.32–36.
[38] 1 Sam 5.3–4.
[39] Ex 28.6f.
[40] Bearing on them the names of the Twelve Tribes of Israel: Ex 28.5.
[41] St. Paul the Apostle.
[42] Gen 49.11.
[43] Galilee: 1 Kg 15.20.
[44] The Sheep Gate being the symbol of Christ: Jn. 5.2.
[45] 2 Tim 1.5.

Wrap the wings of your purity around me, like a royal robe,
And establish in me an unshakeable faith.

My Lady Mary—
Golden Candlestick,[46] six-branched on either side,
Whose summit was crowned with the shape of a flower
And whose base was hammered from shining gold.
You are the Sign of the Covenant, appearing like a fine cloud,[47]
Stretching out your hands before the Father of Mercy, quietening
    his anger.
You are the holy place where Melchisidek made his offering,[48]
He who foretold the Mystery of Justice[49] with three loaves and
    wine.
You are the heritage which Abraham longed for as an old man,[50]
And the mountain on which Isaac was rescued,
When his own life was redeemed by the ram trapped in the thorn
    bush.[51]
You are the grace of the noble Jacob, who saw the Ladder lifted up
    high.[52]
You are the priestly vestment, skillfully woven of fine fabrics,
And studded with gems on its surface,[53]
Woven from different colored strands, set with twisted strands of
    gold.[54]
You are the altar whose surfaces was overlaid with gold,
That held the radiant incense.[55]

[46]Ex 25.31.
[47]Gen 9.12: the rainbow is the "Sign of the Covenant."
[48]Gen 14.18.
[49]The Eucharist.
[50]Gen 15.1.
[51]Gen 22.13.
[52]Gen 28.12.
[53]Ex 39.2.
[54]Ex 39.15.
[55]Ex 37.26.

You are the strength that bore up Joshua, when he rooted out the
    Anakim,[56]
The Hidden Hand which fought against Amalek.[57]
You are the salvation of Deborah, and the strength of Barach's right
    hand.[58]
O Lady, who are more fragrant than the rose by the wayside,
Whom the prophets of Israel contemplated from afar,[59]
You are like the golden full moon,
Or like the dawn, just showing in the East.

O Gracious Lady, this day I pray to you,
From an upright mind, and with all my heart,
Do not allow me to fall into the hands of my enemies.
Snatch me out of the hour of temptation, and from unforeseen
    troubles,
From the day of testing and stress.
And when, at the end, your Son shall come, shaking the very earth,
Allow me to be carried, like an infant in your arms,
Into the everlasting wedding feast,
Into that Age where the joy never fails.

My Lady Mary—
You are the music of that glorious hymn
Which Jacob sang to the righteousness of God,
Which teaches wisdom to children, and knowledge to the young.[60]
You are a sacred book, chased in hammered gold,
Filled with pages of pure purple.[61]
You are the gate, from which came forth the Son of Justice,[62]

[56]Josh 11.21.
[57]Ex 17.16.
[58]Judg 4.14.
[59]Heb 11.13.
[60]Prov 1.4.
[61]The "Codex Purpureus," mentioned here, is a purple-dyed page with gilded text, the most sacred Byzantine form of a liturgical book.
[62]Mal 4.2.

And in his radiance scattered all the darkness of sin,
And with his warming rays melted the frost of wickedness.
O Virgin, you were the tent of Saul of Damascus.
But who could ever number all your many titles?
To tell of them would beggar the most acute intelligence.
One would need to be swifter than the racing horse, speeding over
    the plains,
Making sport even amid the flying arrows;[63]
And even so, one would hardly attain to the terms of your glory.
Even that eagle, which is the spiritual intelligence,
If carried on the back of the Holy Spirit,
After a long flight to the sublime reaches of your heavenly glory,
Could only descend to earth exhausted,
Unable to describe the journey that had been taken.
Even the spiritual sailor, rejoicing in the power of his strength,
Symbolized in those great ships of Tarshish, that went down upon
    the depths,[64]
Even if he peered into the abyss of your love
Could never fathom the sea-depths of your purity.
O Holy One, you are my festal garment, when beforehand I was
    naked.
I shall wear upon my head the diadem of your mercy
And I shall put around my neck the torc of your love.
I pray to you with unshakeable fidelity,
Grant to me the grace of your Son,
And make me his true companion.

---

[63]Job 39.19–25.
[64]Jon 1.3–4; Ps 107.23–26.

*I*n the name of God the Father, who made you the bearer of the
    jewel of his heart,
And in the name of God the Son, who veiled himself with your
    flesh,
And in the name of God the Holy Spirit whose wings came over
    you in greeting,
I sing to you my Lady Mary, a sweet song and a graceful poem.
Once more I bring you the fruit of my lips.[1]
O Bride, since you were always devoid of carnal knowledge,
And since you were the shelter of the Father of Lights,[2]
You are rightly named the Dove;
For you brought good news with the wondrous fresh branch.[3]
You are called the Turtle Dove;[4] and the Queen Bee that gives pure
    honey.
You are called the Ark, to whom the Cherubim offer their shade.
You are the Table carrying the oblation and the holocaust.
You are called the Dish, brimming with milk.[5]
You are called the Chalice of wine, that brings joy to the heart.[6]
You are called the Purification, and the hyssop of sprinkling,
Which sanctifies that which is sordid, and purifies that which is
    defiled.[7]

O Virgin, the proper celebration of your purity
Is beyond the ability of this stammering tongue.
If I were full of knowledge and abounded in wisdom like
    Solomon,[8]

[1]Heb 13.15.
[2]Jas 1.17.
[3]Gen 8.11.
[4]Song 2.12.
[5]Judg 5.25.
[6]Ps 103.15.
[7]Ps 51.7.
[8]1 Kg 4.29.

Or if the spirit of Elijah was found once more in me,[9]
As it was in Elisha when he cleansed the blemishes of Naaman
    with his word,[10]
Or if like Sutael I could drink a river the color of fire,[11]
Or if the branches of my understanding extended and spread to
    the ends of the earth,
And if all my hairs and all my bones were to be turned into
    spiritual tongues,
Or if the pen of my mind were truly exercised in the art of
    composition,
Even then I could not possibly reach the limit of your appropriate
    praises,
For they are greater even than the number of the stars, or the drops
    of falling rain,
And no one can ever count them or estimate them.

O Virgin who brought forth the stems[12]
Bring me safely through precipitous lands, and through the
    dangerous place.[13]
Make me your companion, the fellow traveler at your side.

My Lady Mary—
Bearer of the Sun of Justice
Whence he brought forth his glorious beauty,
And let his rays shine out upon the whole heaven's circuit.
You are the sacred vestment, the vesture of the High Priest
Which he wore in the sanctum when he prayed
For his own sins and those of the people.[14]

---

[9] 2 Kg 4.2.
[10] 2 Kg 5, throughout.
[11] 4 Esd 7.6–9.
[12] Num 17.2; Is 11.10.
[13] 4 Esd 7.6–9.
[14] Lev 9.7.

You are the Tabernacle of the Most High,[15]
The House of the Wisdom of His Son,
Above which the sound of his voice issued forth and was heard,[16]
And where the Cherubim meet one another with touching
    wings.[17]
You are the medicinal pool, in which the sick wash themselves,
Those who lie in the portico of faith.[18]
You are the net cast out into the vastness of the sea of this world,
Which the fishers stretch out to capture the fish of souls.
You are the prize of all our race; and give reward even to the
    animals.[19]
O Virgin, because of you the sorrowing are made merry.
The oppressed are liberated; those who are dead come back to life.
Those who are lost are found again by you,
And those who are far off are brought near.[20]
Those who have fallen are drawn up once more by the rope of your
    love.
Those who have been scattered, you draw together again.
Those who are oppressed find and discover their peace in you.

O Cloud, the raindrops of your compassion water the desert hills,
And the shrubs in the wilderness are refreshed.
Because of your dew, the trees of the orchard flourish and give
    fruit.
O Virgin, you are the winepress of the vintage of rejoicing,
And the spring of the water of happiness.
By your assistance deliver me from the distress and the troubles of
    this age,

[15]Ex 40.35.
[16]Ex 30.6.
[17]Ex 25.18.
[18]Jn 5.2f.
[19]Ps 35.6.
[20]Eph 2.17.

And grant me to recline at the wedding banquet of your Son
In the company of his faithful who multiplied the gold talent.[21]

My Lady Mary—
Tabernacle of Belseel and Ooliab,[22]
Covered with the cloud and robed in the splendor of fire,
You are the Candlestick facing North, and the Table facing West.[23]
You are the Ark, not made by any human skill, but by the Holy
    Spirit.
You are the basin,[24] not made by an artisan, but by God himself,
Which with the water of sanctity and purity, made ablution for all
    the filth of sin.

O Granary of Joseph,[25]
You are the Benediction which made Gad greater.[26]
It was you who conferred the consecration on Levi,
And enriched the treasury of the King of Judah.
You are the priestly robe of Aaron that tinkled with bells.[27]
O Ewe-Sheep, Mother of the Spiritual Lamb,
The Archangels praise you, the Heavenly Powers glorify you.
Turn your wise and knowing eyes upon me;
By your ready help and your righteousness, make me wise.
Let me suck at the breast of learning;
And then I shall expand on the praises of your kingdom.
Engrave on the tablets of my heart the life-giving precepts of your
    Son.

[21]Mt 25.22.
[22]Ex 31.2.
[23]Ex 26.35, according to the Ethiopic text. The Hebrew has the orientations described differently, but the Ethiopic is more apt, since the Table facing West symbolically looked towards Africa.
[24]Ex 38.3.
[25]Gen 41.47.
[26]Deut 33.20.
[27]Ex 28.31–35.

My Queen, be ever quick to help and deliver me.

Encompass me with a defense[28] and guard my life.

Preserve my days that remain, and in your righteousness comfort
    me.

My Lady Mary—

You are the pleasant Mandrake of the Land of Laban

Which Reuben, the first-born of Israel, found in the time of
    harvest,[29]

Which the mildew could never blight, and the arid winds could
    never wither.

You are the Myrrh of Tarshish[30] and the frankincense from
    Sheba,[31]

So sweet the perfume, across the length and breadth of the world,

From East to West, from the North to the South.

You are the chosen Rod, which blossomed with Almonds,[32]

And which gave the people of Israel a prefigurement of you.

You are the Pool of Siloam,[33] and the Cedar of Lebanon.[34]

The branches of your praise shall reach out to the ends of the earth,
    and to the sea.[35]

O Bride, in you the sister of Solomon rejoiced,[36]

She whose breasts were beautiful.[37]

The one whom, after Oholah and Oholibah,[38]

Your Son espoused to himself.

[28]Ps 33.8.

[29]Gen 30.14.

[30]The great sea-going nation of traders (Phoenicians).

[31]Is 60.6.

[32]Num 17.2, 8.

[33]Jn 9.7.

[34]1 Kg 7.2: of which the House of Solomon was built (the type of Mary as the House of Wisdom).

[35]Ps 79.12.

[36]The figure of the Beloved in the Song of Songs.

[37]Song 4.10.

[38]Types of Samaria and Jerusalem, who played the harlot: Ezek 23.1–4.

In you the heavens rejoice[39] and tell forth your majesty,[40]
And the earth is glad, and all those who dwell within its fullness;[41]
The Mountains leap like rams and the hills like nursling lambs.[42]
The sea dresses herself out in your honor,
And the rivers thunder out your praises like applause.
In you righteousness and mercy have found one another,
Justice and faith have embraced.[43]
O Virgin, vessel of pure milk,
Quench the flames of my sadness
And allow me to drink from the fountain of your love.
mercifully protect me from the distress of the time of testing.
Since I have made offering to you of the remainder of my life,
Then be its guardian.

My Lady Mary—
More perfumed than honeysuckle, or the fragrance of myrrh;
More delightful than Topaz, more beautiful by far than Chrysolite,
For inviolate you gave birth to God.
Those on earth give you glory; the angels in heaven rejoice in you,
The chorus of Seraphim praise you, the host of Cherubim proclaim
    you,
For you gave birth to the Spiritual Lamb.
Now grant to my heart a spirit of wisdom and understanding
And put a guard on my lips.[44]
May your protection ever guide me, and your assistance keep me
    safe.
Deliver me from evil, and set me free from tribulation.
O Mother, hear my voice, and listen to my cry.[45]

[39]1 Chr 16.31.
[40]Ps 18.2.
[41]Ps 24.1.
[42]Ps 113.4–6.
[43]Ps 84.11.
[44]Ps 140.3.
[45]Ps 129.2.

My Lady Mary—

Your name runs with milk and honey.

You are ready like the bee to offer good things,

But your disposition is merciful, like the dove.

The Father made you ready as the dwelling place of his Son

Before ever the earth was made,[46] or the vault of the heavens was
set out on high,

Before the sun had ever risen, or the brightness of Orion could be
seen,

Before the rivers ran, before the waters of the Negev were gathered
in.[47]

You are the gift of blessing to Shem,[48]

The grace of Jacob's beauty,[49] the column of witness for Joshua,[50]

The portion of Caleb's inheritance.[51]

You are the Ark, placed between two Cherubim.

You showed your wondrous works in the land of the Philistines[52]

When they led you around (what loss to the house of
Abinadab!)[53]

When they offered you their votive offerings of pure golden
figures.[54]

You are the Golden wall, the Heavenly Sea of Crystal, whose price
is inestimable.[55]

You are the Golden Pitcher, by which means the water of wisdom
was drawn from Horeb.

You are the winepress, that gushed out the wine of gladness,

---

[46]Prov 8.22.
[47]4 Esd 4.54.
[48]Gen 9.26.
[49]Ps 46.5.
[50]Josh 24.26–27.
[51]Josh 15.13.
[52]See *Kebra Nagast* 80. Miracles of the Ark in the land of the Philistines, who had captured it, are paralleled with the miracles of Mary for the Christian people.
[53]2 Sam 6.3.
[54]1 Sam 6.1–4.
[55]Rev 4.6.

The Chaste wedding, all immaculate, the Bride Inviolate.
O Wise Virgin, I knock at the doorway of your halls.
Open to one who seeks, that I may find.[56]
It is your grace I long for, do not withhold it from me.
My heart's desire is to be sheltered by your right hand,
That my foes may never seize me, like the hungry wolf, or the
     ravenous bear.

My Lady Mary—
Consecrated to virginity from your earliest years,
Whose heart gave no entry to the desires of this world,
There is none among men or angels that can compare with you.
You are the thorn bush that bore the flames of fire,[57]
Out of which God himself spoke
About how he would deliver the tent of his people Jacob from it.
You are the Cloud of Manna raining down at the time dew
     descends
All manner of delightful food, flavored according to each one's
     taste.[58]
You are the Basket of Figs spoken of in the prophecy
Which the Ethiopian Ebed Melek found in recent times
When he awoke after a sleep of sixty-six years.[59]
O Virgin, in you God set the seal on the vision of the prophets,
For in you the gates of Paradise were re-opened, which the
     Seraphim were guarding.[60]
Your works are truly wonderful,
But cannot be easily explained to those who question them.
Blessed is he who in your name offers a shout of acclaim,[61]

[56]Mt 7.7.
[57]Ex 3.2–5.
[58]Wis 16.20.
[59]Reference to the Apocryphal *Remnants of Baruch* 5.
[60]Gen 3.24. Though here it is the Cherubim that are given this task, Patristic hymnography and Byzantine iconographic tradition attributed the role to the Seraphim.
[61]Ps 88.16.

Blessed is the one who day by day offers praise to you unceasingly.
Blessed is he who is guarded by the protection of your prayers.
Evil will never harm him, the time of tribulation will never fall
    upon him.
The crowds are no terror to him; he will have no care for the
    uprising of enemies.
The time of testing does not cast him down,
And the hour of affliction does not distress him.
O Queen, who exude such sweet perfume, far and wide,
Grant to this supplicant who seeks a reward
A double share in the riches of your Son, for they can never be
    counted.
Under your wings protect me, and spread your shade above me.[62]

[62]Ps 16.8.

In the name of God the Father who chose you as his spouse.
And in the name of God the Son who was pleased to be incarnate
of you,
And in the name of God the Holy Spirit who made you his Ark,
To you, my Lady Mary, I compose this ancient tale
And for you I sing this new song.

*J*USTLY are you the beginning of the creation of this world,
For you are at once the foundation and the gateway of the whole
endeavor.
O Dawn which knows no eventide,
It was on your account that God created the heaven and the earth,
The sea and its depths, the sun, the moon and stars,
The times and seasons, the winter and summer,
Days and sabbaths, festivals and jubilations,
All the worlds, whether visible or hidden.

O Queen, allow me to tell a few things about your many miracles.
Pour into my heart the oil of the unction of your love
That it might fill up the lamp of faith, and the light of my spirit,
Until the radiance of its brightness shines out clearly through my
lips.
O Holy One, Adam offered the perfume of your magnificent glory
When he mixed the four incenses of myrrh, frankincense, balsam
and nard.[1]
It was also on your account that Enoch set out his benediction.[2]
O Holy One, that bore the sacred fruit,
Multiply the fruit of these my lips, a hundredfold and more.[3]
My Lady Mary—

[1] Ex 30.34–35: The biblical text refers the offering to Moses.
[2] Book of Enoch1.1.
[3] Heb 13.15; Mk 4.8; Mk 10.30.

Royal litter of the New Solomon,[4]
And his ivory throne, with the golden arms.[5]
Before you eleven times nine angels fall down
Who constantly attend in your service, never departing from you
And all the while magnifying your glory, and praising your
      greatness.
Kings serve you, bending their heads before you.
Around you stand princes girded for battle.
O Virgin, you were the grace of the word spoken by Zerubbabel
In the presence of the King and his ministers
When he overcame by his argument the two overseers.[6]
You are the straight highway of God, which Hosea praised at the
      end of his prophecy.[7]
You are the one who took Amos from the flock[8]
That he might convict erring Jacob of its threefold and fourfold
      transgressions.[9]
It was you who fulfilled the prediction of Micah,[10]
For it did come to pass that God was found in you,
A sacrifice more acceptable than thousands of rams.[11]
You are the fount of the benediction of Joel.[12]
You are Mount Zion, the mount of Obadiah's salvation.[13]
You are the mountain on which God appeared.
You were the guardian of Jonah's life, and it was you who led him
      from the bowels of hell.[14]

[4]Song 3.7.
[5]1 Kg 10.18.
[6]Ezra 5.2–17.
[7]Hos 14.10 (LXX).
[8]Amos 7.15.
[9]Amos 2.6.
[10]Mic 5.2.
[11]Dan 3.40.
[12]Joel 3.18.
[13]Ob 1.17.
[14]Jon 2.3.

You are the balsam for the wound of Nahum,[15]
The tower of prayer for Habbakuk.[16]
It was you who fulfilled the vision of Zephaniah[17]
And you who were the ornament of the Temple of Haggai.[18]
You are that rock of righteousness with the seven facets, for
    Zechariah,[19]
And the Advocate of Joshua on the day he received the angel.[20]
You are the House of purity Malachi spoke of[21]
You are the Gate of the Sun of Justice, with healing in his wings.[22]
O Merciful Lady, who gave birth to the Father of Lights,[23]
Ever guard me in his grace, and confirm me in his mercy.
Drive from me the evil spirits of darkness, the lords of this present
    age[24]
Lest they undermine the foundations of my faith.
Never let them destroy the walls of my life, as if it were a paltry
    structure.

My Lady Mary—
Daughter of Heli and Matthat,[25] whom the Powers of Heaven
    praise,
You are the Ark containing the twin tablets,
Whose covering was of the purest gold.[26]
You are the altar of incense[27] ringed with the engraved gold band.

[15]Nah 3.19.
[16]Hab 2.1–2.
[17]Zeph 3.14–17.
[18]Hag 2.7–9.
[19]Zech 3.9.
[20]Zech 3.6–7.
[21]Mal 3.1.
[22]Mal 4.2.
[23]Title of Christ in Jas 1.17.
[24]Eph 6.12.
[25]Lk 3.23–24.
[26]Ex 25.10.
[27]Ex 37.25–26.

You are the dove mentioned in the prophecy[28]
For you are devoid of all trace of anger.
O Good One, for this I trust in that goodness of yours.
Rise up and help me, gird yourself in power in order to save me.
Deliver me from the enemy, and save me from the seductive
    woman.[29]
Wheresoever I go, may you go also; where I abide, may you
    abide.[30]
Sustain me with the food of your blessing; with the wine of your
    love for drink.

My Lady Mary—
Daughter of Matthatha[31]
Heights of purity, and twice sealed in magnificence of life.
You are Bethel, the gateway of the heavenly place.[32]
You are the marvelous stone, over which the holy place there was
    built.[33]
You are the Portico of the Sanctuary, whose arrangement was
    directed from heaven,[34]
And the beauty of whose construction could not be described in a
    single telling.
You are the House in the field which Sutuel was afraid to approach
When he saw it shining like the lightning before him.[35]
You are Bethlehem of the Land of Ephrata,[36]
You from whose womb the great king of Israel came forth as light,
Making the light of wisdom shine forth, and the revelation of
    prophecy.

[28]Ps 67.13–14.
[29]Prov 2.16.
[30]Ruth 1.16.
[31]Lk 3.31.
[32]Gen 28.19.
[33]Gen 28.18.
[34]Ex 27.8–9.
[35]4 Esd 10.25–27.
[36]Mic 5.2.

You are the sister of the daughter of Zion, another heaven,
The strength of heaven and the foundation of this age.
You are the gate of heaven and the way of life, O Virgin,
The help of all in trouble, and the feeder of the orphan.
Grant me a dwelling place in the house made ready for the
    wedding guests,
And love me as a mother loves her own son.

My Lady Mary—
Chalice decorated with pure pearls,
Vessel for the most delightful drink,
Which is the blood of the Lamb
That avoids the dizziness of the vine;
Not like the blood of Abel crying out for the vindication of
    blood,[37]
Or the blood of the circumcision of Zipporah's son,
That was shed in the lodging house,[38]
And not like the blood of Naboth the Israelite.[39]
Rather, a pure blood that remits sins and makes the dying come to
    life.
You are the Table of the Heavenly Bread,
Which is broken for the redemption of many,[40]
And not like that table where the fat of breast and thigh[41]
Was offered by Levi clad in the purple ephod.
O Virgin, make the evil and deceitful spirit draw back from me
And pour out over me the flood of the Holy Spirit
Which reveals the secrets of wisdom,
Conferring eloquence, remedying all defects of expression,[42]

[37]Gen 4.10.
[38]Ex 4.24–25.
[39]1 Kg 21.1–14.
[40]Mt 20.28.
[41]Ex 7.8–32.
[42]Ex 4.10.

Which was poured out over the Apostles, at the time of
    Pentecost,[43]
Sp that they could speak in the common tongue of Mede and
    Parthian alike.[44]

O Royal Scepter, which passed from the Jebusites to David,[45]
Deliver me from this despondency of soul into which I have fallen,
And lead me by the way of justice,
Never allowing me to fall away from the paths of righteousness.
Willingly shall I tell of your miracles.
Permit me to swim in the ocean of your love
And from the stormy waves of this age deliver me
As once your Son delivered the son of Amittai.[46]
May my enemies never say to me:
'Where is the help of your mistress?'[47]

My Lady Mary—
Daughter of the elect David
Desired for her beauty by the King of Kings,[48]
You are the Land of All Delight
Which was created before the heavens.
You are clothed as if in a robe,
The mystical vestment of the Threefold Godhead.
You are the southern portico, near the eastern gate[49]
Where he descended who is blessed from age to age.[50]
You are the Ark which rescued all creation
And which came to rest in Ararat on Mount Lubar.[51]

[43] Acts 2.1.
[44] Acts 2.9.
[45] 2 Sam 5.6–7.
[46] Viz., the prophet Jonah: Jon 1.1, 2.10.
[47] Ps 78.10.
[48] Ps 44.12.
[49] Ezek 44.2.
[50] 2 Cor 11.31.
[51] Book of Jubilees 5.28.

You are the sign of the covenant[52] which was called the 'Bow of
    Cloud'
Making the flood rains of anger hold back from overwhelming the
    earth.
You are she who drew the blessing from Ham and Japhet
And passed it to Shem, who thereby became great.[53]
You are that Oak tree near the tents
Where the three Lords took rest in the shade.[54]
It was on your account that Lot was rescued from the rain of fire
    and brimstone
When God overthrew the great city of Sodom.[55]
You are the Mount of Redemption
Where Isaac was saved from the knife.[56]
You are the almond wood,[57] and the rod of fragrant resin
Which Jacob placed in front of the water troughs[58]
That the flock might breed in wondrous manners.
You are the sacred vestment[59]
With breastplate and humerals
Which the High Priest wore
Whenever he went behind the holy veil
Bearing purest incense, and the blood of a bull.[60]
Elect Lady, you were the hope of our earliest fathers
For by your intercession they were redeemed and snatched from
    distress.
On your account, they passed from death to life.
O Virgin, foundation stone of all happiness,
The choir of angels sings your praise

[52]The rainbow: Gen 9.13.
[53]Book of Jubilees 8.21; Gen 9.26.
[54]A patristic type of the revelation of the Trinity: Gen 18.4.
[55]Gen 19.
[56]Gen 22.13.
[57]Num 17.2, 8; Jer 1.11.
[58]Gen 30.37–39.
[59]Ex 28.6.
[60]Lev 16.12.

With one accord, unceasingly crying:
'Blessed are you above all women,
And blessed is the fruit of your womb,[61] the Lord of Lords.[62]
Exalted Lady, you are exalted far above the patriarchs
And more honorable beyond compare than the prophets.
Your greatness stands out like the moon, and shines like the sun.
It is terrible and awe-inspiring, like an army coming forth in battle
    array.[63]

You are the flower of the field, the lily of the valley.[64]
O sea of purity, the place where all wickedness and sin can be
    washed,
Enclosed all around with gates, and wrapped in cloud.[65]
O Elect One, your honor existed from the beginning
Before the world was made or its regions,
Before the cave of the winds was opened,[66]
Before thunder ever crashed, or gave forth its lightning flash,
Before the land of Paradise was ever established,
And before the beauty of the flowers ever appeared.
I sing your praises not with earthly tongue
Or lips that can give out truth or lies as case may be,
Rather with a pure mind and an open heart.
Thus I extol your wonders, and celebrate you with praise,
Whether I am in the fields, or at home, resting or journeying.
For all day long, in every moment you help me.
Protect me from the enemy who rises against me
And from the terror of dreams by night.[67]

[61]Lk 1.28.
[62]Rev 19.16.
[63]Song 6.10.
[64]Song 2.1.
[65]Like the enclosed garden of Song of Songs (Song 4.12), and the Gated enclosure of the Temple (Ezek 40.4–40), and the cloud-wrapped mountain of Horeb (Ex 19.16).
[66]Book of Enoch 18.1.
[67]Ps 90.5.

Help me avoid the snare of the fowler[68]
Like a bird that has flown the trap,[69] or a deer fleeing the snare.

My Lady Mary—
Tabernacle of Saul who was the teacher of Titus,[70]
The High Priest of Heaven made you his dwelling place
When he laid his ineffable deity in your flesh,
Which the choir of the Seraphim cannot touch
And the ranks of the Cherubim cannot look upon.
But he manifested his grace and mercy in you
And because of you he showed forth the first-fruits of redemption.
With your mediation he brought the rebellions of enemies to a
     standstill.
Take from me desire of the delights of this present age
And do not allow me to draw near
To that which would cause my eye to sin.[71]
Rather grant to me the ability to fulfill my vows,
And accomplish what is pleasing to you.

[68]Ps 90.3.
[69]Ps 123.7.
[70]Heb 9.11.
[71]Ps 118.37.

In the name of God the Father who granted you a royal crown in
*   heaven,*
*   And in the name of God the Son, whom you carried in your womb*
*   for nine months,*
*   And in the name of God the Holy Spirit, who so favorably directed*
*   your path,*
*   My Lady Mary, I bring you this extensive gift of praise.*
*   I offer you this weave of song in full measure.*

KEENLY do I offer you these abundant fruits of praise.
O Virgin, in your presence I pour out my cries, and multiply my
    prayer:
Grant to me peaceful days, long years of mercy.
Never shut against me the gate of your mercy.

My Lady Mary—
you are the enclosed garden,[1] whom no one has opened.
Your breezes scatter the most delightful perfumes.
You are the secret bower of Solomon
The Mount of Sion, upon which descended the dew of Hermon.[2]
O daughter of the wedding feast, number me with your chosen
    ones
Who bring forth the abundant fruit of your Son's righteousness,
When they sit rejoicing, as lords in his palace.

My Lady Mary—
Tabernacle of Light, not sprinkled with the blood of animals,
Multiply this tiny seed[3] of song in the field of my heart,
Let its roots grow deep, and its branches long.
Beseech your Son, that I might come to you cleansed of my sins;

[1]Song 4.12.
[2]Ps 132.3.
[3]Mt 13.32.

Do not forget to visit me, and talk with me most graciously.
Make my life upright, and grant prosperity to my steps.[4]

My Lady Mary—
Sacred vestment a span in width, a span in height,[5]
My soul invokes you, crying out from the inmost heart.
May your lips breathe their sweet perfume into my mouth.[6]
And may the oil of unction be rubbed on my limbs . . .
. . .[7]
May the palm dates be multiplied.
And may your eyes, so full of joy,
Be to me merciful and compassionate.

My Lady Mary—
You are the garden of Cassia and aromatic blooms.
Trembling I pray to you, saluting you with praises.
Receive me kindly, speak to me graciously,
And allow me to remain under the shade of your gladness forever.

My Lady Mary—
Wooden ark that was salvation from the flood's deluge,
And Paradise of delight in which was found all manner of fruit
    tree,[8]
You are the splendor of the Sun, and the radiance of the Moon.
O Mother of the High Priest,
Whose vestments were sprinkled with the blood of divinity[9]
To you have I lifted up my eyes[10]
Crying out in the time of distress:

[4]Prov 13.21.
[5]The high priestly Ephod: Ex 28.16.
[6]Song 7.8.
[7]A line of the poem has been lost at this point.
[8]Gen 2.8.
[9]Is 63.1.
[10]Ps 122.1.

Lead me by your mercy and your abundant peace
Into more stable times, and into length of days.[11]

My Lady Mary—
Lovely Dove,[12] full of reverence,
You are the key of the gates of Paradise.
I praise you with song, I extol you with salutation.
O Paradise of Delight, how I long to take your blessed fruits,
Like the eager bee making my long looping flight in the spirit,
That I can gather into the cellar of my heart, the honeycomb of
    your love.
O blessed Mother of God, turn this rough clatter of mine, into pure
    song.

[11]Ps 21.4.
[12]Song 1.14.

In the name of God the Father who endowed you with grace and beauty.

And in the name of God the Son, who was fed with milk from your breasts,

And in the name of God the Holy Spirit who set you as the Pledge,

I extol you, My Lady Mary, who are called the Candlestick.[1]

*L*IGHT unfailing you allowed to dawn upon us.

Let me tell again of your wonders with fitting faith,

Each one in their proper season.

O Virgin, the First-made[2] gave forth a prophecy about you,

Virgin who are the foundation of our life.

You are like the single grape from the whole vine, that has survived for us.[3]

It was because of you that we were freed from the slavery of the Law;

Through you that we were freed from the dominion of death.

The circumcision of Abraham the Just, brought nothing useful to us,

Nor did the sacrifice of Isaac bring us any benefit.

But through your righteousness we were brought to life.

O Virgin, speedily accept this sacrifice of praise, this incense of prayer,

Which I offer to you, and lay it in the basin of the Seraphim,[4]

Just as the priest lays incense on the live coal in the thurible.

My Lady Mary—

You are the breastplate of the High Priest[5] joined at the shoulders,

---

[1] Zech 4.2.

[2] Gen 2.23: Adam.

[3] The image of perfect humanity.

[4] The Seraphim carrying the incense bowl which holds the prayers of the saints: Rev 5.8, 8.3.

[5] Ex 28.4.

Encrusted with precious stones, arranged for their color and
    beauty
And also to make a regular pattern.[6]
You are the shell of the Pearl of divinity,
Whose discovery exceeds all other things in value.[7]
The riches of the whole world would not approach its worth.

O Elect Lady,
You are the witness to the liberation of the world,
As granted by His Father,
The Ark of the Covenant that was made with the man of peace.[8]
You are the little cloud the prophet spoke of[9]—
Though small, it powerfully fulfilled the word he had spoken.
O Bride, my heart is burning with the heat of the fire of your love.
My heart has left its normal place.
It is leaping for you, so happy it is.
In time of sorrow, it finds its consolation in you.

O Virgin, though it is my desire to swim across the sea of your
    praises,
And tell of all your wonders,
Yet my strength is exhausted as soon as I leave the shoreline.
For no one can gather the winds together in his lap,
Or hold the abyss of waters in the palm of his hand.[10]
Even the great ones of this world, who tried to tell of your praise,
Could not achieve their end or complete the task.

O Light of Beauty, you are the splendor of the Sun,
And the charming gracefulness of the moon.
When your Son, the King who hold the highest power,

[6]The Ephod used in the High Priest's oracular offices.
[7]Mt 13.46.
[8]Noah: Gen.5.28.
[9]1 Kg 18.44.
[10]Cf. Is 40.12.

Shall come again and sit upon his throne of judgment,[11]
Then place me at your right side, and grace me with his light.
For you are the vestment of glory for all his saints.

My Lady Mary—
You shine with more brightness than Melkeya which is called
    Tamayani,
Which has its reign for the quarter year.[12]
You were the soul's life for the son of Barach[13]
And the length of days of the husband of Edna.[14]
You were the ark, the place of refuge for eight souls[15]
When the earth came to rest after the violence of the angels that
    afflicted it.
You are the mountain of the King[16] which he built before Tanim,
And which Caleb the son of Jephunneh took for himself.[17]
You are the sacred Ephod of the judgment of the High Priest,
Which Samuel assumed after Eli, Phineas, and Ophni.
You are the vine of Gethsemane;
Better by far than Lebanon, and more beautiful than the land of
    Egypt.
O Queen, mother of the Redeemer King,
Guard me as the pupil of your eye,[18]
Shelter me under the shield of your mercy.
Deliver me from the mouth of the wolf and from my enemies
Who are far stronger than I.
And snatch me far from the tumult of men,

[11]Mt 25.31.
[12]Namely, the Vernal Sun: see the Book of Enoch 82.15–16.
[13]Enoch, who lived an immortal life: Book of Jubilees 4.16.
[14]Methuselah, Enoch's son: Book of Jubilees 4.27. Methuselah is known as the oldest man in the entire Bible—though he died before his father (who was caught up alive into the heavens!).
[15]1 Pet. 3.20.
[16]Hebron: Num 13.23.
[17]Josh 15.13.
[18]Ps 16.8.

Covering me from the wagging of their tongues.[19]
Sustain me so that I will not falter; strengthen me with your right
        hand.
You who are so happy, turn my sadness into rejoicing.[20]
Take away my sackcloth and gird me with joy.
Reconcile me with your Son
An return me to his grace, both now and forever.

My Lady Mary—
Tabernacle of the desert of Sinai,
Which was overshadowed with glory, and covered with clouds
Wherever the children of Israel went, your people,
You are the Ark which was sheltered by the Cherubim.[21]
O Virgin, radiant in purity and sanctity,
Elect Spouse, most highly pleasing in deed and in fragrance,
Be the medicine of my body, and the remedy for my soul.
Grant me the portion of your benediction, more delightful than
        Manna,
Which eye has not seen,[22] but which the soul has indeed perceived.
O Good One, may the sound of my prayer come to your ears
May it pour itself out before you like fragrant perfume.

My Lady Mary—
White dove from the desert of Barnea[23]
Your clemency is boundless, your gentleness without limit.
The magnitude of your piety is infinite, your good deeds so
        immense.
May the portico of your mercy protect me from malicious
        tongues.[24]

[19]Ps 30.21.
[20]Ps 29.12.
[21]Ex 37.7.
[22]1 Cor 2.9.
[23]Num 32.8.
[24]Ps 30.21.

Cast off from me the chains of sin, and deliver me from slavery.
O Bride, allow me to come to your wedding feast, and do not let
    me be cast out,
Rather let me recline in the company of your elect.

My Lady Mary—
Daughter of the King Hesebon[25]
Clad in golden vesture, adorned with the crown of beauty.
You are the holy of holies,
In which was kept the ark and rod of Aaron the priest.[26]
You are the priestly pectoral made with skilful craft
In which were set the four ranks of gemstones.[27]
You are the land of grain and wine[28]
The garden of fig and dark red apples.
O Virgin, in the gateway are the daughters of the princes
But you are the sole delight of all the faithful.[29]
Come most honored One, like the terrible lion from his cave,
Or like the fearsome leopard from the mountains.[30]
Come Queen, mother of the triumphant martyrs,
And true reward of confessors.
Come Dove from the distant woodland of Paradise,
From the branches of the new olives,
Come Blessed Seat of Glory, ready for peace,
Come Elect One, with your rejoicing companions[31]
The Church of the First Born,[32]
And with all those who kept watch[33]

[25]Ps 44.14, according to the Ethiopic version.
[26]Heb 9.4.
[27]Ex 28.16.
[28]Deut 33.28.
[29]Song 3.11.
[30]Song 4.8.
[31]Ps 44.14.
[32]Heb 12.23.
[33]Images of the Church, like the true disciple (Mt 24. 42), and the wakeful virgins (Lk 25.11–13).

That you may rightly save me from the hands
Of those who practice wickedness in this age
And in the age to come, from the hand of Satan
And his savage demons, who drag off souls behind the gates of
    hell.

My Lady Mary—
Sacred vestment of the priestly humeral,[34] liturgical robe
Made with interweave of gold and purple blues,[35]
It was on your account that God showed grace and remembered
    his covenant
That he did not reject Jacob, and did not cast off Israel.
You are the Gate of Clemency, the Doorway of Salvation.
You always hear the voice of whoever calls out to you in faith.
O Merciful Mother, when the King, your Son,
Shall come again in Judgment,
Then safely receive me on the terms of your covenant,[36] and do not
    cast me out,
But pray to your Son for me,
That he may not turn away from me the glance of his compassion.
Be my comfort then to take away my fear,
And bear me up lest I should fall.

[34] Lev 8.7.
[35] Ex 28.6f.
[36] The *Kidan* of Mary: the tradition in the Ethiopian Church that the Blessed Virgin Mary made a pact with her Son that part of her eschatological glory would be the fact that she could gain the final salvation of any who, while on earth, honored her by word or deed. The *Kidan*, of course, was one of the chief motives of the liturgical composition and recitation of this poem.

In the name of God the Father who from on high came down to
strengthen you,
 And in the name of God the Son who was made man from you,
 And in the name of God the Holy Spirit who came to overshadow
 you,

*M*Y Lady Mary—
I shall speak of your holiness and, one by one, shall tell of your
 wonders
Which are the delight of angels and the joy of humanity.
O tender heifer[1] who bore the fattened ox
Sacrificed to forgive the sins and transgressions of the world[2]—
You are the closed door[3] through which no one entered and no
 one has left
Other than the Lord of Hosts, your Son,
Who raised up once more the House of David
And who is our Protector and Helper.
And if that enemy who prefers hatred to peace,
Should raise up against me the wicked tumult of his attacks
And secretly snare me with his traps
Then gird me round with strength[4] and give me the victory
Never me allowing to fall into the power of his hands.

My Lady Mary—
Gate of the Sun of Righteousness[5]
You are the Chariot in which he appeared
And the cloud of glory with which he was covered,
He whom the stars of Orion are dazzled by.

---

[1] A biblical term of endearment; see Jer 46.20.
[2] Ex 24.5; Heb 10.12.
[3] Ezek 44.2.
[4] Ps 17.33.
[5] Ps 18.6.

O Queen, because of you,
Those who were far off now draw close once more[6]
And through you the scattered are gathered in, and the sick made
    whole;
The deaf are made to hear again,[7] and the dead to rise up.[8]
Through you the mute learn to speak words of peace;
Through you the waves of temptation are stilled
And the winds of wickedness are made calm.
O City of Salvation, in you rejoice all those who go out early[9]
And you are the exultation of those who come in at Eventide.[10]
O Virgin, you are the oil of the Kingdom's Lantern,
By your prayer save me from devious men who stir up strife
Who speak sweet words while secretly fomenting war,
Who outwardly give marks of affection
While inwardly they seethe with hate.[11]
May they be speedily cut down by the sword.[12]
May they fall as once did the walls of the tower of Babel,[13]
Or as the tower of Siloam was undermined.[14]
May they be scattered as the dust of sand[15]
And vanish like the smoke of an oven.[16]

My Lady Mary—
Mother of the Victorious God
Himself unseen, but seeing all,

[6] Eph 2.17.
[7] Cf. Mt 11.5.
[8] Both symbolically (sinners are returned to grace) and also in reference to the Ethiopian books of the Miracles of Mary, which recount in great detail the continuing works of the Theotokos in the world.
[9] Ps 125.6; Sir 32.14.
[10] Ps 64.9 (LXX).
[11] Ps 27.3.
[12] Ps 62.11.
[13] Gen 11.1–9.
[14] Lk 13.4.
[15] Cf. Ps 1.4, 17.43.
[16] Ps 36.20.

You are the adamantine wall which no aggressor can ever scale;
You are the foundation of our hope for reward[17]
And very reward that the laborer hopes for.
It is you who make those far off draw close once more,[18]
And gather in the scattered.
Whatever is hard to bear you make light, assisting all who are lost.
O Exalted Lady, you lift on high the wretched of the earth
And raise up the poor from the dust.[19]
Hear now my cry[20] and listen to my appeal.

My Lady Mary—
Virgin within and without,
If all the abysses of water in the wide expanse of heaven
Or throughout the vast space of earth
Could be turned into ink
It would not be enough for any man to write down all your titles of
   honor.
O Virgin, let your ears be attentive to the sound of my voice[21]
And let your lips pass on to your Beloved Son,
That Lord of Mercy, the prayer of my mouth.
Pray for me that he would deliver my soul
From the snare of men's tongues.[22]

My Lady Mary—
Twice-clothed,[23] dressed in mysteries,
You gave birth in virginity to the Conquering Lion of Lions.
O Virgin, through you the bubbling temptations are stilled
Through you the power of the waves of rebellion are quietened.

[17]Job 7.2.
[18]Eph 2.17.
[19]Ps 112.7; Ps 33.7; Lk 1.52.
[20]Ps 5.2.
[21]Ps 129.2.
[22]Sir 51.3.
[23]Prov 31.22.

O Queen, may I never be as a man without an Advocate[24]
But deliver me from despair
And since you are my Patron, save me from ruin.
Protect me under the shadow of your grace
From all who speak against me[25]
And hide me in the hallways of your graciousness.
Put upon me the mighty hand of your Son
Which is a terror for all enemies, and cows the foe,
That it may crush the violent man, and bring the envious to
        nothing.

My Lady Mary—
Mother of the Lord God,
You are the Sister of Angels, and the glory of the mortal race,
Whose glory differs from that of all other creatures.
Your heart overflows with immense clemency.
Your name is the wine of rejoicing
Your beautiful face is like the breath of perfume.
Your love is like a bubbling spring in a hot and thirsty land.
O Daughter, you are the Mother of the Anointed Nazarene,
Who makes known was hidden, and reveals what was secret.[26]
My prayer to you is that you allow me to dwell in the land of
        abundance and peace.

My Lady Mary—
Horn of that unction of purest balsam
Which was made by the mixing of four kinds of perfumes,[27]
You are the welcome shield of salvation,
And the warrior's armor.
Now O Virgin, may the words of my mouth be heard by your
        heart.

[24]Ps 87.5.
[25]Ps 30.21.
[26]Lk 12.2.
[27]Ex 30.34.

And if my enemy has turned against me, inciting rebellion,
May your word of rebuke fall upon them speedily
Crashing down upon them like the waves of the sea.
May they wither and dry like the grass on the roof,[28]
And dry up like a root.[29]

[28]Ps 128.6.
[29]Ps 102.11; Is 40.24.

*In the name of God the Father who consecrated you as his
    tabernacle
    And in the name of God the Son, who slept on your lap
    And in the name of God the Holy Spirit who added purity to
    purity upon you,*

NIGHT and day I beseech you
My Lady Mary—
And reverence you on bended knee.
Now, O Virgin, speak to your Son and say:
'Hear the prayer of your mother, my Son,
And be mindful of your mercy and your kindness.
And do not enter into judgment with your servant.[1]
For the sake of your name[2] do not call to mind the sins of this
    sinner.
O my Firstborn, be mindful of your goodness
And strengthen him with your word,
And make him worthy of your wedding feast.
Allow him to dwell with your elect on Sion, your holy mountain.'

My Lady Mary—
Golden Couch of Solomon[3]
All the creatures of the world bend their knee before your
    greatness,
And offer praise and blessing to your glorious name.
O Bringer of Life whose greatness the prophets of Israel foretold,
Fulfill my soul's deepest prayer, and my heart's desire,
And grant that if the violent principalities of darkness[4]
Which lord over this mortal world[5]

[1] Ps 142.2.
[2] Ps 24.11.
[3] Song 3.9.
[4] Eph 6.12.
[5] Jn 14.30.

Should in their pride rise up to work my ruin
Then come to my assistance, as one friend would help another
    friend,
And guard me for ever under the care of an angel of your Son.

My Lady Mary—
Mother of God, Mother of Our Ruler,
Daughter of Joanan and daughter of Melchi,[6]
You who wear the vestment of sanctity, and are clothed in the
    purple of purity,
Bride of royal lineage, who blossomed from the priestly rod,[7]
You are the Treasury, and the pearl of great price.
There is nothing that remotely approaches your beauty.
O Elect Lady, to what beautiful or desirable thing could I ever
    compare you?
For your praises are unequalled.
See I knock at the gate of your house. Open to me,[8]
That I may enter into your sanctuary
Where the elect of your Firstborn recline.
Protect me from the whispering of those who accuse and slander[9]
And from the tongue of the proud who find fault in your praise.

My Lady Mary—
Throne of the vision of Barach[10]
Whose appearance lends color to the sapphire,
Whose face has the radiance of alabaster,
You are a heavenly palace, the royal mansion in this land.
You are the Ark of the Commandments,
Designed by the hand of the Creator[11]

[6]Lk 3.27–28.
[7]Num 17.8.
[8]Song 5.2.
[9]Ps 43.17.
[10]Zech 6.13.
[11]Ex 25.10.

On top of which there were the Cherubim and the golden overlay.
O Bride, radiant in splendor and light,
When your Son prepares the festive banquet for his elect
Place me then at his right hand, as your servant.

My Lady Mary—
Who bore the King,
Your glories are like the tributes from the land of Tarshish,[12]
Like gold and precious stones, or topaz from the land of India.
O Virgin, I have become the herald of your greatness,
And so I will magnify you with praise[13] and exalt you with
    blessings.
O Elect Lady, calm for me the terrible whirling of the winds
Lest they blight the shoots of my life, like dry roots,[14]
Or like a mallow that withers and fades.[15]
But send me your protecting grace, and kindly help.
This is what I have hoped of you.

My Lady Mary—
Who gave birth to the heavenly King,
Whatsoever you do, is the best that can be,
And diffuses the odor of Cassia.[16]
I salute you, as once the angel Gabriel did, saying:
"Hail, you who are blessed above all women;
Blessed is the fruit of your womb."[17]
All shall bless you, all shall bend the knee before you.
Seven times a day I praise you,[18] telling of your goodness,[19]

[12] Ps 71.10.
[13] Ps 68.31.
[14] Ezek 17.9–10.
[15] Job 24.24.
[16] Cinnamon-smelling bark of the aromatic tree.
[17] Lk 1.42.
[18] Ps 118.164.
[19] Ps 70.15.

From late at night to the break of day, from morning to evening.
Save me from the drawn bow of hostile lips,
And from the arrow of the hostile tongue.[20]
Preserve me from distress and save me from calamity.

My Lady Mary—
Blossom of the Rose of Jericho,[21]
I sing of your womb,
I load with blessings your mother's lap
For there he took his little seat who is the God of all.
I narrate your wondrous deeds, and tell of your goodness.
O Holy One, it is not earthly goods I seek as reward,
But grant me rather your righteousness,
And the gift of your peace in addition.

[20]Jer 9.8.
[21]Sir 24.17–18.

In the name of God the Father who desired your beauty,[1]
   And in the name of God the Son who was incarnate of you,
   And in the name of God the Holy Spirit who decked you with the
      purple of purity,
I offer you, my Lady Mary, this pleasant song of praise.
I bring before you the pleasing sacrifice of salvation.

O VIRGIN you are the Ladder of Prayer,
And the Stairway of Intercession.
I name you the Garden that brings forth aromatic herbs.[2]
I name you Summer and Spring, the time of flowers.
I name you the Sea like the purest crystal.[3]
O Gentle Lady, see how I lift up the eyes of my heart to your help.[4]
Let your ears be attentive to the voice of my pleading.[5]
May the sound of my voice be acceptable in your sight
And do not allow me to be the sport of demons
Or to fall into the hands of my enemies.

My Lady Mary—
Rod which grew up from the root of your father David,[6]
Our fathers have told us of your miracles
And once more I recount them in due order and sequence.
May the salt of your lips give flavor to my mouth.
For you, O Virgin, are the Gate of the Sun and the chariot
That moved him from the furthest ends of heaven
To the threshold of the boundaries of this world.[7]

[1]Ps 44.12.
[2]Song 4.12–14.
[3]Rev 4.6.
[4]Ps 122.2.
[5]Ps 87.3.
[6]Is 11.1.
[7]She moved the Infinite Word, that is, an incomprehensible distance, to be incarnated in time and space.

You are the orchard garden and its pleasant aroma,
You are the fragrance of perfumed spices.[8]
In you heaven and earth rejoice;[9]
In you mankind and angels become one family.
Because of you the Patriarchs of former ages
Made their way to the immortal city.
Save me from my enemies, who in their arrogance make plots
    against me.
By the power of your prayer, set them to flight.
May they be uprooted as once they were in Endor.[10]
Let them descend into the abyss of perdition
And fall into the pit of destruction.
May they fall to the sword, and be encompassed by their
    enemies.[11]

My Lady Mary—
Mother of the Life-Giving God
Daughter of the King of Judah, and daughter of Levi the priest,
You are the Gate of that Sun who rises at dawn
Exulting like a giant, rejoicing like a Bridegroom.[12]
You are the fleece of Gideon's great miracle[13]
The Strength of Samson the Nazirite.[14]
O Virgin, it is through you that the whole lineage
Of the ancient generations is made known,[15]
And in you most marvelously is shown the mystery of rebirth.
My Lady, lock up the door of my heart, with the key of your love,
And light the lamp of wisdom in the house of my soul.

[8]Song 4.12–14.
[9]Ps 95.11.
[10]Ps 82.11.
[11]Ps 62.11.
[12]Ps 18.6.
[13]Judg 6.39–8.29.
[14]Judg 13.5.
[15]Mt 1.1–17.

Wherever I abide, may you abide. Wherever I go, may you go,
     too.[16]
Night and day be at my right hand
And ever save me from the hand of the wicked man
Lest he seize me like a lion,[17] or like a famished bear.

My Lady Mary—
You are the paradise of Adam and Eve,
Sevenfold perfumed in its plants; a garden of aloes.
By your intercession the captives were brought back from the
     valleys of judgment.
You are the daughter of Perez who was the son of Tamar[18]
(Not the daughter of Selah which was Sua).[19]
You are the grace of Judith the Betulian[20]
Which she had against the Assyrian prince[21] and his servant the
     eunuch Bagoas.[22]
You wear sanctity about you as if robed in real silk.
Now my Lady, by your help
Make straight the paths of my life,
And say to him who is the fruit of your womb:
"For the sake of your own self, forgive the transgression
Of this creature, because he is weak,
And there is no man who understands his sin.
But receive the voice of his prayer,
Overturn the counsel of his enemy[23]
And throw away his sin as if it were a stone
Cast aside into the abyss of your compassion."[24]

[16]Ruth 1.16.
[17]Ps 7.3.
[18]Gen 38.1–6, 29.
[19]The difference being God blessed the former lineage but not the latter.
[20]Jdt 8.11.
[21]The Assyrian prince is Holofernes: Jdt 11.20f.
[22]Jdt 12.12.
[23]Viz. Satan, at the Last Judgment; cf. 2 Sam 15.31.
[24]Is 38.17.

My Lady Mary—
You are the column of testimony for Joshua son of Nun,[25]
For the God of Hosts was glad to assume your flesh as his vesture
    of glory.
You are the Ship of salvation, the beams of the Bridge of Justice.
You are the document of freedom for those who languished in
    slavery.
Because of you they came to rest after their servitude,
Because of you they were snatched out of their tribulation.
Because of you the son of Amittai was saved,[26]
And the Ninivites gloried in your mercy.[27]
Grant to me your grace, and your life-giving peace.

My Lady Mary—
Your name is aloes and myrrh
Whose perfume is richer than granulated incense.
You are that House of Glory built upon the palanquin of the Living
    God,[28]
Whose seat was made of snow white ivory.[29]
Exalted mother of the Living God,
Save me always from the lies of deceitful men[30]
And ever protect me under your wings
For they are to me a solid shield of proven worth.

My Lady Mary—
You are the field of the King of the Valley of Shaveh[31]
Which God promised to Abraham
And conferred on him as an inheritance for his descendants.[32]

[25]Josh 24.26–27.
[26]Jonah.
[27]Jon 2–3.
[28]The Litter of Solomon: Song 3.7–10.
[29]The Throne of Solomon: 1 Kg 10.18.
[30]Ps 42.1.
[31]Gen 14.17.
[32]Gen 13.15.

You are the bread and wine which Melchisidek then brought out.[33]
O Virgin, because of you God was made manifest, and was made
    man,
And willed to be incarnate within your womb,
For your purity pleased him greatly, and thus he desired your
    beauty.[34]
O Queen, I pour out my heart before you[35]
For when I fall down before your mercy
Mercifully do you hear me, accept me, and respond.

[33]Gen 14.18–19.
[34]Ps 44.12.
[35]Ps 61.9.

In the name of God the Father who strengthened your right hand,
  And in the name of God the Son who wrapped you in the cloud of
    his divinity,
  And in the name of God the Holy Spirit, who made you his altar,
  I bring to you, My Lady Mary, a tribute of measured praise,
  Like an offering of innumerable coins, each one inscribed with
    your name and face.[1]

$\mathcal{P}$RAISE I bring you as the fruit of my lips[2]
A blessing which my mouth has spoken and my mind has
      conceived,[3]
As I consider the symbols that have been spoken and revealed
      about you.
Ewe sheep that gave birth to the Lamb,
Reverently do I serve you,
Seven times a day I recite your praise.[4]
With all my heart I pray to you, most earnestly do I beseech you,
O Mother, do not permit the eloquence of my mouth to be cut off
Rather open for me the four gates of the wind[5]
Which brings gracious peace when it blows.

My Lady Mary—
Mother of the Lamb of God
Which John saw in the midst of the Seven Lamps,[6]
When we was caught up into heaven, and called out to give
      witness.[7]

[1]Mt 22.20.
[2]Heb 13.15.
[3]Cf. Ps 44.2.
[4]Ps 118.64.
[5]Cf. Book of Enoch 76.4. Here, a symbol of inspiration.
[6]Rev 1.13.
[7]Rev 1.2.

You are the City of Refuge which the Elders of Israel established[8]
So that anyone could flee to it,
And exiles could find protection there, in you.
Princes speak of your peace,
And the Kings of the earth rise up to praise your kindness.
The poor and needy find a place of honor with you.
By your might the exhausted are able to regain their strength.
The mute sings out the greatness of your praise,
Tales which celebrate you, which even the deaf can hear.
O spring of delight, fount of running water,
How the spirits of darkness flee from the radiance of your face!

My Lady Mary—
Daughter of the priest Aaron,
You are the tree which the force of the devouring flame could not
        hurt,
For the fire was inextinguishable, but the bush was not consumed.[9]
Moses saw you[10] when he was pasturing the flock of Jethro.
Philanthropic mother of the philanthropic King,
You lend your gracious ear to the cry of all creatures,
So, now, snatch me from the hand of the wicked oppressor.

My Lady Mary—
Decked in beauty, radiant in your wedding garments,
Emitting a perfume more fragrant than myrrh or aromatic spices,
The ninety books of the Law speak throughout of your praise,
Especially those which Sutuel described, in the number of forty
        days.[11]

[8]Josh 20.2.
[9]Ex 3.2.
[10]Ex 3.1: The Burning Bush is a patristic typology for the Blessed Virgin who, just as the bush impossibly contained fire within it, so did she impossibly contain the fire of the Godhead within her womb. To this extent, as Moses saw the Bush, so he saw the Virgin in a prophetic type.
[11]Cf. 4 Esd 14.37. In 4 Esd 14.44, the author says he has written ninety-four books.

You are the wedding hall, the house of delightful rejoicing.
Give me the Spirit of your Son, who is the strength of my soul
And grant me a share at the banquet in the halls of wisdom.

My Lady Mary—
You are the crystalline vase of the unction of joy,
The Glass of the wine of rejoicing.
The sound of your voice is sweet[12] to the ear like dropping honey.
It was on your account that God instituted the passage of the days
    of the week[13]
When he made the world by his word.
O Queen who gave birth to the Benefactor of all,
I have made you my mother; make me now your servant.
I have established you as my delight, the staff that holds me up,
And so I pray to you, my Lady, take from me
The veil of ignorance, and the film of sin.
Strike the war horses of my foe with blindness and fright
Confuse their riders, and render them captive.

My Lady Mary—
You are the mount of Horeb, place of judgment and justice
Where the terrifying clamor of trumpets was heard,
The crashing thunder and the awe-inspiring voice.[14]
You are the chalice containing the holy wine[15]

The Ethiopian canon was considerably larger than that of any other church but the reference to the ninety and forty probably derives from this obscure reference to 4 Esd.

[12]Song 4.3.

[13]A rabbinical tradition stated that it was on account of the beauty of the Torah, pre-existently conceived by God, that the Creator made the world. Here the author sees God finding in the beauty of the Theotokos a motive not only for his own entrance into creation, but for the whole conception of the world order. There is also a sense intended that the week, as it is liturgically conceived as a way of dividing up the praises of Mary in the churches, finds its true fulfillment.

[14]Ex 19.16.

[15]Perhaps the Grail from the Mystical Supper is meant, but probably the cup of drink offerings from the Temple sanctuary; cf. 1 Macc 1.22.

And [the finely woven curtains] of the Tent of Witness.[16]

You are the casket of the law, decorated with the four rings of gold.[17]

You are the candelabrum giving light, with the seven lamps upon it.[18]

You are the rod of the priest Aaron with the living almond blossoms.[19]

O Virgin, through your ready help

Grant that the enemies ranged against my life

Will die off like the flower of the field,[20] be crushed to pulp like a reed.

My Lady Mary—

In humility I praise you, and sing to you as a supplicant,

For you are the altar of the high priest.

I am one who, with faith, eats the bread of life of your Son,

And who listens to your child, of sweet memory, with the ear of his heart.

So now say to your Son on my behalf:

"Give to this my servant effective grace.

Help him with your right hand, and purify him in justice.

Gird him with dread that he may strike down the enemies of his life."

---

[16]Ex 26.1. This line and part of its predecessor is textually corrupted.
[17]Ex 25.12.
[18]Ex 25.37; Zech 4.2.
[19]Num 17.22.
[20]Ps 102.15.

In the name of God the Father Who anointed your body with the
*   balsam of purity and sanctity,*
* And in the name of God the Son, who made you his vesture,*
* And in the name of God the Holy Spirit, who put over you his*
*   shining glory,*
* I offer you, my Lady Mary, this sweet psalm of song,*
* And offer you this fragrant smelling oblation of sacrifice.*

QUEEN, you are the Ark that carries the commandment[1]
You are the bridge that lets me cross the precipice,
And allows me to pass over the waters[2]
Holding on to the rope of your love.
Grant that within my heart may rise that star of grace,
The star of the Holy Spirit.

My Lady Mary—
You are the vesture of the high priest,
Crown of gold upon his head, and miter of his perfect beauty.[3]
O Fountain of honor, you set forth the spring of the river of life.
Those who are thirsty drink from you,
Those who are in sorrow are consoled by you.
You are the city of abundance in which the just rejoice
And in which those who once were sad are now filled with
    gladness.
You are the staff of faith, by which the elect are supported,
And the righteous borne up.
O Virgin, ask of your Son, that he might free me
From the fearful sea of tribulation, whose waves never seem to die
    down.

[1]Ex 25.16.
[2]4 Esd 7.6–9.
[3]Sir 45.12–13.

My Lady Mary—
Mother of the Omnipotent God
Who worked wonders in Bethsaida,
And showed his might in the region of Chorazin[4]
You are the generous daughter of the most gracious King,
Overflowing with all goodness, full like a river in torrent.
You are the gentle dove that never quarrels or fights—
Stretch out your pure wings and cover my heart under them.
Command the angels of mercy ever to establish their camp around
    me.[5]

My Lady Mary—
Mount of prophecy, covered on all sides with fragrant trees,
As is described in the Book of Enoch,[6]
You are the Golden Ladder of the region of Luza
Which the young man, full of the Spirit, saw in the night.[7]
You are the Tabernacle of Testimony, covered with the cloud of
    glory
Whose portals were ten, all interconnected.[8]
You are the Ark that came back from the land of Gaza
And into the house of Abinadab.[9]
Rising swiftly, as if on wings,
Come to my help that I may pass over the precipice
And safely cross the abyss.[10]

My Lady Mary—
Purest one always, and throughout all time,

[4]Mt 11.21; Lk 10.13.
[5]Ps 33.8.
[6]Book of Enoch 24.
[7]Jacob: Gen 28.12.
[8]Ex 26, throughout.
[9]1 Sam 7.1.
[10]4 Esd 7.6–9.

In you have I placed my trust from the beginning even to the
    present hour.
You will be the hope of my life, from now and to the ages.
O Virgin, you it was who gave birth to the Lord of All,
Whose wisdom, like a river in flood, fills the four corners of the
    world.
O Virgin, come to my assistance without delay,
Draw near to me for my consolation.
For my enemies say about me: "How long before he dies?"[11]
Let calamity fall on them instead, and their hopes be dashed.

My Lady Mary—
Palace of the High King
Whose timbers were of cypress and whose beams were of cedar,[12]
You are the Holy of Holies, the place of judgment and precept,
Whose wooden panels were covered with the finest gold they
    could find,
While over it there stretched the wings of the two protecting
    Cherubim.[13]
You are the pectoral vestment and humeral of the priestly robe,[14]
Made of carefully woven plaits, and fastened with golden rings.[15]
You are the altar of incense[16] and the bowl of the fragrant thurible.
Yours is dominion, yours is majesty.
Always be present to me in the day of tribulation and distress
Like a beloved sister, like a friend giving consolation.

My Lady Mary—
You are the crystalline vase of sweet-smelling balsam
That delights the heart as much as it pleases the senses.

[11]Ps 40.6.
[12]Song 1.17.
[13]1 Kg 6.22–23.
[14]Ex 28.6.
[15]Ex 28.13.
[16]Ex 37.25.

The King of Kings himself desired your beauty[17]
And clothed himself in the cloud of your flesh.
To you I sing in gladness of heart;
I make my prayer to you in times of sadness.
Whenever the cup of sorrow disturbs and darkens my heart
Be close to me as my comforter,
Come to me in your gracious and consoling presence.

[17]Ps 44.12.

In the name of God the Father who chose you,
And in the name of God the Son who appeared in your flesh,
And in the name of God the Holy Spirit
Who poured out over you the riches of his grace,
To you, my Lady Mary, I sing the good psalm of this song.

RIGHTLY do I sing to you with all my might,
For you have been my help since my youth.[1]
You were my consolation while I was still within my mother's
    womb.[2]
O Virgin, imbued with the aroma of saffron,
Graciously accept my song of praise
And sign upon me the mark of your service.[3]
May those who plot against my life, and find me an irritation,
Never be able to delude me.
Let them never find cause to rejoice over me.
Let them be broken and cast down instead.
May they be famished and go begging for bread;
May their prayer be held as a sin;
May their appeals be reckoned as blasphemy.[4]
May they follow the flight of the swine and drown in the abyss.[5]

My Lady Mary—
Daughter of Matthat and Mathatha[6]
Prophets with inspired eye were able to gaze upon you in the spirit
Giving partial revelations[7] in the form of pleasing figures.

[1] Ps 70.5.
[2] Cf. Ps 70.6.
[3] Cf. Gal 6.17.
[4] Ps 108.7.
[5] Mt 8.32; Mk 5.13.
[6] Lk 3.23–24; Lk 3.31.
[7] 1 Cor 13.9.

You are the heaven of God[8]
You are the chariot[9] in which he was accustomed to appear
And the cloud of glory wrapping his immensity.
The Cherubim supplicate you
The Seraphim sing of your royal dignity.
The hordes of St Michael fall down before you.
The hosts of St Gabriel venerate your glory as supplicants.
O Virgin, deep gulf of the sea of mercy,
And vase of the unction of peace,
Save me from enemies who plot malice against me.[10]
May they fall into the pits which they themselves have dug.[11]

My Lady Mary—
Blessed arbor, most lovely among the trees,
It was you who brought forth the flower of faith,
And bore the berry of all benediction,
Ever fresh, never withering.

Because of you the slave has something to eat.
Because of you the freeborn live in blessedness.
O Bride, you are more splendid than Benasse,
More beautiful by far than Toma.[12]
Ever show in me the efficacy of your saving help.

My Lady Mary—
Daughter of Judah, and daughter of Leah
Who made her way from the Mesopotamian
Euphrates to the land of Syria.[13]
You are the Gate of Spring, the month of rejoicing.

[8]Ps 113.23.
[9]Ps 67.18, etc.
[10]Ps 34.4.
[11]Ps 7.16.
[12]Ethiopian names for the Moon and the Sun: see the Book of Enoch 78.1–2.
[13]Gen 31.4f.

O Virgin, how I long for your grace, and desire your help.
Do not let the whirlpools of this frightening
Sea of tribulation submerge me,
But let your prayers be a ship for me
And your intercession my little boat.

My Lady Mary—
I have commanded my tongue to sing the praises of your name
And to pour out prayers of supplication in the portico of your law.
I have dedicated myself as your man,
The servant of the praise of your majesty,
Because you gave birth to the King of Mercy,
Who is the High Priest who remits all sin.
O Virgin, pray to him for me, that he may be my benefactor,
Dismissing my faults and not scorning my petition.

My Lady Mary—
Mother of the Lord God Adonai,[14]
How delightful it is to tell of you,
How pleasant to call you to mind.
For you are as lovely as the sound of the harp,
Or the songs of the tavern.[15]
O Virgin, save me from the wicked man[16]
Whose ways are those of evil, and whose paths are crooked.

My Lady Mary—
You are that pectoral vestment which was said to be "deeply
        rational"[17]
Which was woven with plait and metal work

---

[14]*Adonai* ("My Lord") is title of the Most High in the Hebrew Bible; here, it attributed to the Divine Logos.

[15]Where secular love songs could be heard.

[16]Ps 139.2.

[17]Ex 39.1; namely, made with great craft. In patristic diction, "rational" also meant "spiritual."

And upon which were set the precious stones laid in alternating
    series,[18]
The vesture of Aaron which he wore on the solemn festivals
When he appeared before the Lord,
And when he passed behind the sacred veil to make the sacrifice of
    expiation.[19]
O Bride, you are the dove of prophecy.
Whenever I pray to you, making ceaseless intercession,
Be near me without delay.
As a reward for my song
May I have what mind has not thought of,
And what has not entered into the heart of man.[20]

[18]Ex 39.10.
[19]Lev 16.12.
[20]Paradise: cf. 1 Cor 2.9.

*In the name of God the Father who anointed you with the balsam of
    his name,
  And in the name of God the Son, who was born from you,
  And in the name of God the Holy Spirit who made you his tower,[1]
  My Lady Mary—
  I sing the psalm of this song to your faithful friends.*

*S*ACRIFICE I offer to you,
Which is the fullness of praise
Which my heart is able to conceive, and my mind is able to
    perform.
Elect and Pure Lady, you have been made the sister of the angels,
Raised to lofty heights.
The purity of your flesh is like the snow and the frost.
O Virgin, you have been made the firmament of purity,
And the foundation stone of faith.
Whenever my enemies gather against me
Send upon them trembling of the heart, and weakness of the joints,
The devouring sword, the grappling hook that devastates,
The javelin in the field, pestilence in the city.

My Lady Mary—
Daughter of the sons of Jesse,
Who arose from his lineage, and ascended from his stock,[2]
You are the vine root whose four spiritual clusters of grapes
Were of the order who were born of fire.[3]
For you they serve and before your glory they fall down
Honoring you, and praising your sanctity.

---

[1]Song 4.4; Ps 61.3.

[2]Is 11.1.

[3]Cf. Ezek. 19.10–11; here, the four evangelists are meant. The "order born of fire" is the Seraphim, who were seen as the types of the evangelists in the vision of the four animals, in Ezek 1.4–10.

You are the support of heaven, and the pedestal of its columns,
The tranquility of the sea, and the solidity of the earth.
You are Mount Sion, where the dew of compassion[4] springs forth.
You are the sacred breastplate, a span in length and a span in
    breadth.[5]
O Virgin, basin of the sea of mercy,
My enemies, with murderous intent,
Burn with the fire of vengeance they themselves have kindled.[6]
Let them be drowned in the abyss of destruction
Like that herd possessed by madness.[7]

My Lady Mary—
Mother of the Unknown God,[8]
Whose glory is greater than the Cherubim, and vaster than the
    Seraphim,
Who are praised by the Principalities, and venerated by the
    Powers,
You are the Vine of Justice, not the vine of Engedi.[9]
I savor the taste of your grapes in my mouth.
May your mercy follow me all the days of my life[10]
And ever protect me.
May your salvation remain always upon me.

My Lady Mary—
Vesture of the priest Levi, and royal crown of Judah,
The kings of the earth offer you gifts[11]

[4]Ps 132.3.
[5]Ex 39.9.
[6]Is 50.11.
[7]Mt 8.32.
[8]Acts 17.23.
[9]Song 1.14.
[10]Ps 22.6.
[11]Ps 71.10; Mt 2.11. It is the (traditional) combination of these typological biblical verses which over the course of time rendered the "wise men" of Matthew's Infancy narrative, into the "three kings" of popular piety.

Of red gold and white pearls,
Purest crystal, and that most desirable gem Epomida.[12]
O Bride of Bethlehem, from the region of Bethsaida,
Grant to me days of peace, as many as my soul desires,
Until your Son shall come again to dispense justice and
    retribution.

My Lady Mary—
You contained the burning fire of the deity.
You were made in a different fashion to other women
At least in relation to the laws of conception and birth.[13]
Your greatness far exceeds that of all other human beings.
Elect Lady, you are the boast of the families of Nashon and
    Aminadab.[14]
You are the height of honor for Shelumiel and Zurishaddai.[15]
You are the golden coin of faith.
Open to me, that I may enter in the portal, through the gates of
    your grace,
Just as Rhoda, that daughter of gladness, once opened to Peter.[16]

My Lady Mary—
Daughter of Jesse the Son of Obed,[17]
Whose goodness overflows, whose holiness spills out abundantly,
We creatures of clay offer you our praise,
The host of angels stand in attendance on you.

[12]Cf. Ex 25.7 (LXX). According to Oudenrijn (*Scriptores Aethiopici* 40, p. 67), the Ethiopian tradition rendered this term as the name of one of the most precious stones on the priestly Ephod (not just the name of the Ephod itself).

[13]The Apocryphal traditions of the miraculous conception and birth of the Blessed Virgin, and also a reference to the miraculous conception and birth of the Christ.

[14]Num 1.7; Mt 1.4 (lit. "and Amishad'dai," as in Num 1.12: but it seems to be a slip).

[15]Num 1.6.

[16]Acts 12.13.

[17]Ruth 4.17.

You are the house of glory,[18] the work of greatest delicacy,
Of him who fixed the orbit of the stars, sprinkling them with
        frost.[19]
You are the holy place in the Sinai desert,
Surrounded by clouds, looking as if it were overshadowed with
        fire.[20]
You are the Ark of the Covenant,[21] and the Table of the bread of
        sacrifice.[22]
Speak to me in truth, show yourself visibly,
Then shall the wicked depart and cease their prowling around.[23]

My Lady Mary—
Golden Candlestick[24] of the Son of Iddo,[25]
Shining with bright radiance from the bowl placed on its top,
Which scattered and dispelled the deep gloom of sin;
For this was the light which came down from the bosom of the
        Father
Because he had so desired your beauty,[26] falling in love with your
        loveliness.
This light it was that you bore, even though it was a burning flame,
Carrying its flame within you, as if in the bridal chamber,
And so you were called his Palace.
O Virgin, whose virginity is changeless,
Now, because of the incarnate union,
It is your flesh that sits at the right hand of the Father's power,
Just as the Word sat there immemorially.
When my relentless foe shall rise up against me,

[18]The Holy of Holies.
[19]I.e., starlight.
[20]Ex 40.36–38.
[21]Ex 37.1f.
[22]Ex 37.10.
[23]Ps 9.17, 12.8.
[24]Zech 4.2.
[25]The prophet Zechariah: Ezra 5.1.
[26]Ps 44.12.

And stirs up against me the violent tumult of battle,
Set upon his head the hand of your Son,
To wither his limbs, and bring his strength to naught.

In the name of God the Father, who established you as a river of
*   holiness and purity,*
And in the name of God the Son, who joined his deity with your
*   flesh,*
And in the name of God the Holy Spirit, who so wondrously
*   visited you,*
I sing this song of gladness to you, my Lady Mary,
Joining with the Powers, and blessing you with the Jubilations,[1]
Or like those who were carried on the backs of their mules.[2]

T HE beauty of the dove is yours, a stranger to all malice,
You are for us a fountain of clemency,
An overflowing lake of compassion.
O Bride, be to me a golden torc around my neck, and golden rings
    in my ears.
By the fragrance of your dress, change to a good odor
The foul stink of my sins.

My Lady Mary—
Vine that bears the vintage of life
Which gives joy to the heart and gladdens the mind[3]
And stretches out its branches to the sea, to the very shore of the
    river,[4]
You are the adornment of the High Priest
Worn for the remission of sins, and the forgiveness of trespasses,
When, clothed in it, according to the prescripts of the law,
He passed within the sanctuary.[5]
O Virgin, who are the river that overflows with peace,

[1]"Powers" and "Jubilations" are the names of different ranks of the angelic
order.
[2]Cf. Judg 5.9–10.
[3]Ps 113.15.
[4]Ps 79.2.
[5]Lev 16.12.

Whenever my enemies boldly rise against me,
By your prayers and your assistance
May they be diminished in force and in number.

My Lady Mary—
Blessed tree, which brings forth perfumed flowers
And blessed fruit to eat, whose leaves never wither[6]
Even when the month of Keramt augurs the end of summer.
O Virgin, you are the city, always prepared and fortified.[7]
Remember my prayer, and let it ascend to the presence of your
    Son;
By the fervor of your love lift up my petition on high.

My Lady Mary—
Full of honor and without stain,
In grace and honor you are greater far
Than the hosts of angels, or the whole race of mankind.
It is you who are glorified in the midst of the church[8]
And who are celebrated in the heavenly choir.
The glory that is yours, is given to no other;
It is uniquely yours, of a wholly different order.
O Virgin, may my prayer come into your presence,
Let it be drawn up on high by the rope of your love,
And once it is on high may it always be before you.

My Lady Mary—
First-fruits of the sacrifice of remission,[9]
You are the fragrance of the altar, and the flower of priestly
    anointing.

[6]Ps 1.3.
[7]Ps 47.2, 86.1–2.
[8]See Ps 21.23 (LXX).
[9]The Virgin is the first disciple, the first of the heavenly and earthly church to be redeemed by the saving work of her Son.

You are the ring of encircling gold,[10] the ivory throne of glory,[11]
On which the ram descended, the leader of the flock.[12]
You are the wondrous vestment of the priest, and his linen tunic.[13]
O Virgin, daughter of Nadab[14] and daughter of Naggai,[15]
Accept my supplication, and let my prayer ascend.
Hear me as I call,[16] and lift up on high the sound of my cry.

My Lady Mary—
You are the Ark, made according to the prescripts of the Law,
Whose way was made level through the midst of the river Jordan,[17]
When your people passed over from the territory of King Og.[18]
It was on your account that the land was hushed
And the sound of lamentation ceased.
Ever guard the lamp of my faith from the wind that blows in off the
    sea;[19]
May it never wane, but be like a moon that shines even when day
    has come.

My Lady Mary—
House of prayer[20] and seat of the assembly,[21]
In whose womb the Lord of Hosts[22] willed to be made flesh.
Reap the harvest of my enemies,[23] making them skip like the calf
    of Lebanon.[24]

[10]Ex 25.10–11.
[11]1 Kg 10.18.
[12]The Lamb on his throne, incarnate from the Virgin: cf. Rev 6.16.
[13]Ex 28.42.
[14]Song 7.1, according to the Ethiopic version.
[15]Lk 3.25.
[16]Ps 5.2.
[17]Josh 3.14–16.
[18]Josh 12.4.
[19]The sea of the sorrows of this world.
[20]Is 56.7; Lk 19.46.
[21]Heb 12.22–23.
[22]Ps 23.10.
[23]Jer 15.7; Mt 3.12.
[24]Ps 28.6.

Reduce their hosts to nothing, and scatter the multitudes of their
armies.

In the name of God the Father, who mingled your name with the
*   balsam of his name,*
*   And in the name of God the Son,*
*   Who brought down his Godhead into the arbor of your body,*
*   And in the name of God the Holy Spirit, who covered the Ark of*
*   your womb*
*   In the gold of sanctity and purity,*
*   I come to you for the delight of the perfume*
*   My Lady Mary,*
*   For yours is the fragrance of nard, and spice, and fragrant resin,*

*U*NGUENT such as is mixed together, reserved for the
     consecration of priests.[1]

And . . .[2]

In you God reconciled the world to himself.[3]

My Lady Mary—

You are the city of refuge, where the sons of Israel found safety,[4]

When they ran to you, fleeing from the avenger of blood.

You were the benefactor who provided the price of redemption

As exacted by the Assyrian.[5]

O Holy Tongs which held the burning coal of Godhead,[6]

Into your hands I place the care of my body and soul.

Whenever the violent princes of darkness range themselves against
       me

Grant that they may be shattered like a potter's jar.[7]

---

[1]Ex 30.20.

[2]A line is missing in the manuscript.

[3]Cf. 2 Cor 5.19. In St. Paul, the subject is God the Father; here, it is the Divine Word who chose to reconcile the world in the Blessed Virgin, that is, in the act of Incarnation.

[4]Josh 20.2.

[5]2 Kg 18.13–16.

[6]Is 6.6.

[7]Ps 2.9.

My Lady Mary—
My Shulammite,[8] turn your ear to my prayer
And pour upon my head the oil of anointment.[9]
Fall upon all my enemies from behind with knotted whip
And strike the crown of their head.[10]

My Lady Mary—
Holy Ark that bore the precepts of the Yawta,[11]
You have ever been free from the lusts and desires of this world
And never have they seduced your mind.
O Mother, let the voice of my cry come into your hearing,
And may it return to me, with my heart's desire fulfilled,
The prayer of my soul accomplished.

My Lady Mary—
Everlasting Queen
It was you the Kings of the Medes venerated,
The Princes of Parthia and Elam,
Who came as suppliants to your glory.[12]
O Pure Virgin, virginal within and without,
Strike and lash my soul's enemies with fear.

My Lady Mary—
More fragrant than cinnamon or balsam,
You are the shoot of the perfumed rose,
The jasmine by the seashore.

[8]Song 6.13–7.1.
[9]Ps 22.5.
[10]Ps 67.22.
[11]"Yawta" is the Ethiopic letter that was equivalent to the Greek I, the first letter of the name of Jesus, and bearing the numerical value of Ten (Commandments). The Yawta is the Divine Word, who gave the Law, and was incarnated of the Holy Virgin.
[12]Ps 44.13, 17; cf. Acts 2.9. The episode also recalls the scene in the Byzantine Akathist when the Persian Kings came bringing gifts to the Virgin.

You are that fragrant tree of Enoch, the son of Jared.[13]
O Virgin, Mother of the Mighty King,
By your righteousness deliver me
On that day of silence, when we are rendered dumb,[14]
Just as the righteousness of your father Abraham was the salvation
    of Lot.[15]

My Lady Mary—
You are the bazaar where bargains are found,
Where God bought back the world.
It was on your account he made the heavens,
And separated light from darkness.[16]
Let my prayer come into your sight[17]
Like a perfume poured out
And may it accomplish my desire and fulfill my request.

[13]Book of Enoch 24–25.
[14]The time of death, and the hour of judgment
[15]Gen 18–19.
[16]Gen 1.4.
[17]Ps 87.3.

In the name of God the Father,
Who cast aside the charter of blame from the foundation of his
    Law,
And in the name of God the Son,
Who hid his burning deity in your flesh, as in a quiver,
And in the name of God the Holy Spirit,
Who by his word proclaims both summer and winter,[1]
I fly to you My Lady Mary,
Lest the jaws of the evil serpent should engulf me.

*V*ISCERAL blood of animals sprinkled all around[2]
With purple linen and hyssop fronds,
These are things of the past;
For you are the New Tabernacle,
My Lady Mary.
May all my enemies be transfixed
By the javelin of your help.

My Lady Mary—
Save me from the jaws of the ravenous lion[3]
And from the mouth of the devouring serpent.[4]
Strike the crown of my enemies
With the force of your vengeance.

My Lady Mary—
Daughter of Joachim, the brother of Cleophas,
You are she whose Son forbade the eating of the bat and the
    hoopoe,[5]

[1]Ps 147.15–18 (LXX); Job 38.16–30.
[2]Heb 9.21.
[3]Ps 21.22; 1 Pet 5.8.
[4]Ps 90.13.
[5]Lev 11.19: the Incarnate Word as the Lawgiver of the Old Testament.

Equally, the kite and the gull.[6]
It was you who were the grace
Contained in the preaching of Paul
When he taught before Agrippa.[7]
O Mother, I pray to you,
Grant me the sword of the Holy Spirit[8]
And a quiver full of the arrows of victory
With which to pierce my greatest enemy of all, Mastema.[9]

My Lady Mary—
Greatness of the Kingdom of Heaven,
As once compared to the mustard seed[10]
Under which the birds of Paradise came to find shade
As if they were in the cedars of the gardens of Jaffa.[11]
O Virgin, stretch out your devouring sword
Against the enemies of my soul,
And pierce them with an arrow of perdition.

My Lady Mary—
May all who hold your royal decrees in contempt
Be utterly cast down.
May they fall into the pit of perdition
And be devoured by the mouth of Hades.

My Lady Mary—
Land of best inheritance,
That does not yield the onions and garlic of Egypt,[12]

---

[6]Lev 11.14, 16.
[7]Acts 26.1.
[8]Eph 6.17.
[9]The name of the leader of the demon host: Book of Jubilees 10.18.
[10]Mt 13.31.
[11]Cf. Ezek 31.8.
[12]Num 11.5.

Whoever hates you
May the hand of the great angel strike them down.

In the name of God the Father,
  Who designed your flesh as the dwelling place of his Only Begotten
    Son,
  And in the name of God the Son,
  Who made you his Gateway,
  And in the name of God the Holy Spirit,
  Who fashioned you as his Ark,
  My Lady Mary,
  I proclaim your righteousness
  As it stands written in the scroll of the book,[1]
  And I tell of your indefectible holiness.

WHY does Benasse[2] shine so brightly?
Why does Aryares[3] blaze so radiantly?
If not for you?

My Lady Mary—
That House visited by God,
Whose greatness is inexpressible
Whose beautiful appearance is ineffable,
It was for you that the prophets of Israel
Built up their tower of prophecy.
O Holy One, set me back firmly
In the discipleship of your beloved Son.
Cause my enemies to flee from before my face.
May they be crushed as fine as the dust of sand.[4]

My Lady Mary—
Bride arrayed in all her finery,[5]

[1] Heb 10.7.
[2] The Moon; cf. Book of Enoch 78.1.
[3] The Sun; cf. Book of Enoch 78.2.
[4] Ps 1.4.
[5] Is 61.10; Ps 44.14.

Resplendent like the dawning day,[6]
What gloom of ignorance you dispel!
What veils of error you remove!
What fog of sin you disperse!
Rise now and come to save me.
Crush all the enemies of my soul.

My Lady Mary—
House of the Holy Spirit,
The lights of heaven bow down to praise you.
Your glory is proclaimed at the gates of Sion.[7]
You are the Ark of the Commandments
Which the Creator himself designed with his own hand.[8]
O Virgin, grant that my feet
May ever walk in the way of peace.

My Lady Mary—
Queen of Heaven,
Radiance never setting,
In whom we mark no passing day,
May God who was the architect of your flesh
Ever chastise me with a word of mercy
And correct me with the rod of his love.

My Lady Mary—
You are the lofty throne seen by Isaiah, son of Amoz,[9]
In the year Uzziah died of his leprosy.[10]
You are that House of Glory
Whose walls were built of fiery bricks.[11]

[6]Song 6.9.
[7]Ps 9.15.
[8]Ex 31.18.
[9]2 Kg 19.2.
[10]Is 6.1; 2 Chr 26.21.
[11]Book of Enoch 14.9–13.

You are the Sacred Ark.
The altar of your womb
Was built by God's own right hand.
You are the Inheritance of Israel
Whom God never ceases to visit.
O Holy One, all praiseworthy and immaculate,
Gird me in your justice
Wrapping me as in your robe,
And make me run in the paths of your law.[12]

My Lady Mary—
You are the gateway for the brilliance of the Godhead,
And so, if my enemy looks on me with scorn
May a word from your mouth upbraid him,
And be my salvation.

[12]Ps 118.32.

In the name of God the Father,
  Who made the seed of holiness and purity
  Germinate within your heart,
  And in the name of God the Son,
  Who joined his wondrous Godhead to your flesh,
  And in the name of God the Holy Spirit,
  Who made the theology of your majesty
  Sing out in the mouths of the prophets,
  I make so bold as to compare you,
  My Lady Mary,
  With that bush that wrapped itself in flame,[1]
  And I ask you, O Virgin,
  To wipe the tears from my eyes,[2]
  And take away the stumbling block from my feet.[3]

X

My Lady Mary—
You are the new Noah, surviving the wreckage of the world;
You are the Tree of life
From which the shoots of new creation were begun.
O Good One, ask your Son on my account
That he might never shut to me the gate of salvation.

My Lady Mary—
You are the graceful paradise of delight
Offering all the fruits of life.
Hear me when I call to you[4]
And strike all my enemies with the plagues of Egypt.

---

[1] Ex 3.2.
[2] Rev 7.17.
[3] Ps 90.12.
[4] Line missing here, but this is the sense.

My Lady Mary—
Stranger to all the works of evil,
The praises of your purity would exceed the number of the stars in
    heaven
Or the grains of sand upon the seashore.[5]
Elect Lady, allow me to take a fruit from the branch of the tree of
    wisdom.

My Lady Mary—
You are the vessel of honor,[6]
The treasure which the moth can never consume.[7]
You are the fortified city,[8]
Which no battering ram or axe can ever disturb.
Save me from that fire which never goes out
And the worm that never sleeps.[9]

My Lady Mary—
Thorn bush of the field of Midian,[10]
Whose branches and leaves were bathed in fire,
Be my strong help.
Make sure I do not waver, and keep me from falling.

My Lady Mary—
You who knew no evil,
Whose deeds excel all others,
You are that tower where men take refuge,[11]
Grant, then, that I may never have cause for fear—

[5]Gen 22.17.
[6]2 Tim 2.21.
[7]Mt 6.19–20.
[8]Ps 121.3.
[9]Mk 9.48.
[10]Ex 3.1f.
[11]Prov 18.10.

Neither the terror that walks by night
Nor the arrow that flies by day.[12]

---

[12]Ps 90.6.

In the name of God the Father, who engraved the Ark of your flesh
With the chisel of purity,[1]
And in the name of God the Son, who assumed the cloud of your
flesh,
And in the name of God the Holy Spirit,
Who made you his couch,
I recite for you, my Lady Mary,
A Book of Similitudes.[2]
O Virgin, the greatness of your glory extends to,
And fills up, the very ends of the earth.

My Lady Mary—

Y OU are the vestment of the High Priest,[3]
Grant that my enemies may descend into the pit of perdition.
May they be lashed like the Philistines.[4]
But as for me, save your servant, both now and forevermore.

My Lady Mary—
Tree of Life covered with the foliage of purity,
And clothed in the green of sanctity,
Break the neck of my foes, lash them from behind,
And let not one of them escape from the field.

My Lady Mary—
You are the white dove of prophecy,[5]

[1]Ex 25.11, 25.
[2]Sections taken from the Old Testament used in the Ethiopian Church to recount the praises of the Blessed Virgin, which this poem is emulating.
[3]Ex 28.2–28.
[4]1 Sam 5.1f.
[5]Gen 8.11.
[6]Ps 67.14.

Whose wings had the color of flashing silver,
And whose sides were covered with the purest gold.[6]
O Virgin, overflowing river of purity,
Who have no equal,
Ask your Son to look favorably upon my prayer.

My Lady Mary—
Fragrant girdle of the Deity,[7]
By means of you He purged the world of sin.
May the power of your purity lead me through the fiery lake[8]
And set a guard around me on every side.[9]

My Lady Mary—
You are the fount of glory,
The unfailing spring of compassion,
Where thirsty souls,[10] the world over, come to drink.
You are that close-woven net, mentioned in the Gospel.[11]
Allow my prayer to ascend to you without hindrance
And let it come before your face.

My Lady Mary—
You are the beehive of the honey of the Law,
Over whom the heavenly bee[12] cast the shade of his wings
When your heart perceived the angel's voice.[13]
Grant that I may ever dwell in peace in your wedding hall
In the company of the elect, sharing in your blessing.
This is my prayer; all that I hope to attain.

[7]Cf. Song 1.12.
[8]4 Esd 7.6–9.
[9]Ps 140.3–4; Ex 23.20.
[10]Cf. Ps 103.11.
[11]Mt 13.47.
[12]The Holy Spirit
[13]Lk 1.35.

In the name of God the Father, who blessed and sanctified you,
   And in the name of God the Son, who took his own body from
       yours,
   And in the name of God the Holy Spirit,
   Who made you into a golden vessel of purity and sanctity,
   My Lady Mary,
   I name you as the Bush that was clothed in fire.[1]

Z

My Lady Mary—
Vessel of the Father of Lights,[2]
And vine of Righteousness,
You are the palm filled with dates.[3]
O Virgin, exterminate the enemies of my soul
That not one of their buzzing swarm may remain.[4]

My Lady Mary—
You are the little woven basket[5]
As pure as the promised word.[6]
Be for me a blessing and a sanctification.

My Lady Mary—
In whom there is a double portion of the grace of God,
You are the throne of the Father's glory.
The titles of your honor are more numerous than the stalks of grass
Or the grains of sand on the seashore.[7]
You are the lamp of the Light of Life.

[1]Ex 3.1.
[2]Jas 1.17: title of the Incarnate Word.
[3]Song 7.6–7.
[4]Ex 8.31.
[5]Ex 2.3.
[6]Ps 11.7.
[7]Gen 22.17.

My Lady Mary—
Blessed tree, like to the mustard bush,[8]
You are the little bottle of the ink of the Holy Spirit's quill
Be for me like a helmet of victory upon my head[9]
And the shoe of salvation under my feet.

My Lady Mary—
Who are sister of the angels
And the boast of their mighty throng,
You are the Ark of the Commandments
Over whom the Cherubim stretched their wings.[10]
Elect Lady,
You are the daughter of anointed kings and priests.

My Lady Mary—
The Holy Word made you his own flesh.
And so it is fitting to proclaim you, to bless you,
That your holiness should be the song
On the lips of men and angels.

[8]Mt 13.31.
[9]Is 59.17; Eph 6.13–17.
[10]Ex 25.16–20.

In the name of God the Father who made you wholly for life,
  And in the name of God the Son,
  Who heaped upon you a great abundance of grace,
  And in the name of God the Holy Spirit,
  Who constituted the power of your virginity
  As the hinge on which the door of your holiness and purity turned,
  I pour out my prayer before you as your supplicant,
  My Lady Mary,
  Ewe sheep that gave birth to the Lamb.

*A*LL pure mother[1] of the Immaculate Lamb[2]
Who fashioned man in the beginning,[3]
And forms them even to this day,[4]
To you I make my request, my Lady,
That all around my house may be piled
The teeming bundles of your blessings.

My Lady Mary—
Mother of the All-Making God,
Grant me an abundance of all that is desirable.
Lead me in the path of righteousness[5]
Lest I wander off in the desert of error.
Command that the gate of the house of wisdom[6]
Should ever be left open to me.

My Lady Mary—
Maker of Peace, who have always been a stranger

[1]The Ethiopic language has several more letters than English. Hence the notional device of beginning the alphabeticized sections again with a final AMEN.
  [2]Jn 1.29.
  [3]Gen 1.26–27.
  [4]Jn 1.3; Col 1.15–20.
  [5]Ps 5.9.
  [6]Prov 9.1.

To the noise of argument and squabble,
Cleanse the defilement of my flesh,
Be it as red as a berry, or as black as a crow,
And reconcile my soul to Him who formed and fashioned it.

My Lady Mary—
Who fashioned Him who Fashioned all,
May your blessings never cease to accumulate
All around me as gifts.

My Lady Mary—

MOST beautiful Bride,
Dressed in graciousness and sanctity, as in fine silk,
The full extent of your praises cannot be numbered or estimated.
You are the priestly breastplate[1]
Covered over with the precious stones.[2]
In you the whole world was made new,
After it had grown old and weary.
In you the poor man, who has never longed for precious gems,[3]
Even so becomes rich.
Tower of Defense which fears no grappling iron or battle axe,
Be the defense of my life,
And the fortification of my salvation.

My Lady Mary—
You are the House of shining gold, founded on precious stones,[4]
Whose walls were lined with Cypress,
And whose beams were made of Cedar.[5]
Elect Lady, your kindnesses are without measure
And cannot be numbered.
May they ever be about me
And cover me like a vestment of fine silk.
You are my fortress, and the force of the axe cannot break through.
Free me from the snare and the trap[6]
Which my enemies have laid in secret against me.[7]

---

[1]Ex 28.15.
[2]Ex 39.8.
[3]Especially the ascetics who have dedicated themselves to voluntary poverty.
[4]Rev 21.9.
[5]Song 1.17.
[6]Ps 30.5.
[7]Ps 9.9.

My Lady Mary—
Queen of Heaven,
The delights of this earth were never what your heart sought after.
Renew the power of my life, as a fortress wall can be repaired,
And do not let me fall into the dust.
Do not take into account, and do not remark,
The multitude of my sins.

My Lady Mary—
City of wisdom,
Whose walls are knowledge, whose fortifications are good counsel,
Do not hand over the glories of your riches to a stranger's hand.
My Queen, may it seem pleasing in your sight
That the full account of my sins may not be reckoned.

My Lady Mary—
Full of glory, and wondrous honor,
May the sin of lust not fall upon me grievously,
But rather grant that my body may reverently remember you,
And I may be girded in your remembrance as with a belt.

My Lady Mary—

*E*NERVATION grips my body
For it has begun to stink with the putrefaction of sin.
Give me back my bodily health,
Help me in the day of tribulation,[1] as a sister would help a brother.
O Queen, root out sin from me, as one would uproot a diseased
    plant.
But may their branches wither away who hate my life.
Anoint me with the balsam of your love,
Lest the wounds of sin should ever fester in me.
Elect Lady, may your great peace descend on those who love your
    name.[2]
But may trembling of limb and rottenness in their bones[3]
Fall upon those who hate you.

[1]Ps 58.17.
[2]Ps 68.37.
[3]Prov 12.4.

Epilogue

$\mathcal{N}$ow,
My Lady Mary—
I have played the lyre for you,
The Lyre of Praise,[1] as is fitting for your royal honor.
I have set out my song in the order of the Alphabet,
Following each of the letters in series,
With sections given to each of their vocalizations.
So that it may be clearly manifest to all,
This is how I set about dividing the literary sections.
Those letters which had seven vocalizations numbered twenty-six.
And the minor letters,[2] which I placed at the end,
Were of the number of the hands and feet.
This is my offering to you,
A matter of meters and measures.

O Virgin, great cluster of the living grape,[3]
My Dove,
Not all the sons of men who live
Could ever write the full extent of your praise
Or ever be enough to tell the tale.
Even so, this child of praise, which my lips have brought forth,
Let it spring up in the field of your heart
Like the flower of the fertile meadow.
May it grow, and flourish, and blossom, and turn into spice.

May this silver of my song,
Cast forth from the javelin of my tongue,

---

[1] *Enzira Sebhat*: the literal title of the poem as a whole, although the author in his prologue also calls it the "Harp of Glory."
[2] The consonants and labials.
[3] Cf. Num 13.23.

Be an offering to you of pennies and coins,
And guard it for me in the treasury of your home in heaven.
May it be dear to you,
As a child is dear to its doting father,
Or like a baby on its mother's lap.
As such a babe will never leave its place of rest,
Just so may I never cease to find my rest, reclining on your lap.

My Lady Mary—
Holy One, twice virginal,[4] pray for me
And gain for me the gift of mercy from your Son,
Who so desired your beauty,[5]
That he may not be mindful of my sins
Committed knowingly or unknowingly,
In word or in deed, by hearing or by sight,
Whether by passive agreement, or by action,
Whether through lust, or by being led by vainglory,
Whether a matter of offering insult, or rebellious muttering.
For your sake may your Son truly love me.
Because of this may he have a great honor in store for me.

My Lady Mary—
Holy One, and twice virginal,
Whose name in Hebrew is Maryam,
You are the crown upon my head,
My ornament of great beauty.
From the depth of my heart do I love you
And I cry to you in the time of my distress,
Making a loud appeal, my throat hoarse from shouting,[6]
As often as my enemies say:
How long before he die and his name be forgotten?[7]

[4]I.e., in body and soul.
[5]Ps 44.12.
[6]Ps 68.4.
[7]Ps 40.6.

My Queen,
Hear my call at the dawn of day,
And be attentive to my cry.[8]
What use would it be if I were to descend into the pit?[9]
Should not lips of clay sing to your glory?[10]
The way in which my life shall flourish
Is itself testimony to your justice,
For even I,
Delight of my Eyes,
Shall tell the tale of your justice all the days of my life.

O Virgin,
Accept this grateful song of my lips.
And, to the ages of ages,
Gracefully bless with your reward,

Your Servant,
A deceitful sinner,
Hensa Krestos,
The scribe who wrote all this.

Amen.

[8]Ps 5.2, 4.
[9]Ps 29.10.
[10]Cf. Ps 87.12.

POPULAR PATRISTICS SERIES

ST VLADIMIR'S SEMINARY PRESS
1-800-204-2665 • www.svspress.com